THE ATTIC

A Bur Oak Book

The Attic

A MEMOIR

Curtis Harnack

UNIVERSITY OF IOWA PRESS • IOWA CITY

University of Iowa Press, Iowa City 52242

www.uiowapress.org

Copyright © 1993 Curtis Harnack

Originally published by Iowa State University Press, 1993

First University of Iowa Press edition, 2011

Parts of Chapters 1 and 3 are reprinted from the *New York Times*,
copyright © 1977/82/84 by the New York Times Company,
reprinted by permission. Chapter 4 was originally featured in
Book Forum.

Printed in the United States of America

The University of Iowa Press is a member of Green Press Initiative
and is committed to preserving natural resources.

Printed on acid-free paper

Library of Congress Cataloging-in-Publication Data

Harnack, Curtis, 1927–

The attic: a memoir / by Curtis Harnack.—1st University of Iowa
Press ed.

p.   cm.

"A Bur Oak book."

ISBN-13: 978-1-58729-546-1, ISBN-10: 1-58729-546-6 (pbk.)

ISBN-13: 978-1-58729-966-7, ISBN-10: 1-58729-966-6 (e-bk.)

1. Harnack, Curtis, 1927—Childhood and youth. 2. Authors,
American—20th century—Biography. 3. Farm life—Iowa.
4. Iowa—Social life and customs. I. Title.

PS3558.A62474Z463 2011   2011002350

813'.54—dc22

[B]

Contents

Preface

One's earliest years tend to leave the deepest impressions, and most writers draw upon that stock of primal experience, especially at the start. I found that I could write best about Iowa if I remained physically distant from it, though it was no conscious choice, just the accident of where jobs took me. I always regarded myself as an Iowan who happened to live elsewhere, who returned home as often as he could. The truths one discovers in childhood tend to serve in later settings as well, for it is often said that those who know their own small village know the entire world. My teacher at Columbia, Lionel Trilling, used to say everybody has at least one story in him: it is how I grew up and what I discovered about life.

We Have All Gone Away (1973) was part of that story for me, but of course there's more; there always is. One writes a memoir to discover what recollection of a time or particular event might reveal, seeking to make the personal into something universal to which unknown readers might relate. The process of writing an account is usually a revelation to the author. You may have a feeling of what you want to say, but not until you dig down and pull it out do you know exactly the nature of it. If you are too clearly aware of your viewpoint or have a slant on the memoir before you've begun, it's likely to sound self-serving or not on the level, with perhaps too much special pleading or justification. The reader should feel a participant in the author's discoveries.

Your account might have all the facts and dates right but still be mostly wrong about what matters. Or you might make mistakes in certain particulars but be on the mark in every way that counts. In this important way a memoir is not like history. It can succeed in portraying people and places without having to rely solely on the outward trappings of exactness, though an honest effort must always be made.

After publication of *We Have All Gone Away,* some members of my family took it upon themselves to point out just where I had been inaccurate. I certainly hadn't meant to be; it wasn't fiction. I told what I thought I knew about my Iowa farm childhood. One cousin wrote that my maternal grandfather's family, emigrating from Bern, Switzerland, by way of France, did not lose in Paris the tiny boy who was to be my grandfather. It was his brother who got lost. Therefore, my remark that as children on the farm we used to speculate that if grandfather had not been found by his parents in time to make the boat train, we might have grown up French simply wasn't true. However, the point is it was true to *me* at the time, part of family lore. Every writer of a memoir gives a version, the best of which he or she is capable, even when not all of it can be verified.

In that book I also relate certain episodes regarding the Farm Holiday movement, that radical protest effort during the Great Depression. But I don't know if I actually saw picket lines and farmers dumping milk cans or if I imagined those scenes from the vivid talk of the elders and felt I'd witnessed them. If I consciously know I'm making things up, I'm writing fiction; but if it seems to be the truth and I regard it as such, it's memoir.

Writing autobiography often exorcises a lot of ghosts. You come to grips with things bothering or fascinating you, investigate nagging questions, lay to rest certain wrong notions, or stumble upon new information. By writing it down you arrive at decisions regarding this material, which is the stuff of your being. Therefore, a memoir sometimes frees one from the claims of the past and allows the author to move on. But often when it comes to personal history, nothing is as simple as that.

Anyhow, I found I had more to say. I left the farm decades ago and many changes have occurred. People close to me have died; situations have altered. Leaving doesn't end much if the emotional ties remain. There seemed to be more to the story—and here it is.

THE ATTIC

THE FARMHOUSE, C. 1910

PICTURE A HOUSE

Time once again for a visit home, to the Iowa farm forty miles northeast of Sioux City where I grew up. My ailing Uncle Jack, now in his eighties, lives there alone. For thirty or more years I've been making the pilgrimage to my past from various parts of the country, each time telling myself, probably this is the last.

A few university speaking engagements would help pay transportation costs. Therefore, instead of the usual abrupt arrival at the Sioux City or Omaha airport, I traveled slowly through Iowa, welcoming the dream-pod journey, gently making the transition from who I am now to how it once was for me.

At the bus depot in Cedar Rapids, where I changed coaches, I noticed a queer, stirred look on several faces—the atmosphere felt charged. Then I spotted what it was: a bearded, grizzled man in a blue homespun coat with no buttons, only hooks up the front; a teenage son in a similar rumpled outfit; and a bonnet-clad mother. So, a visit from our ancestors.

I headed for the men's room and discovered a second youth from that archaic family. He held up dripping red hands with a foolish, bewildered grin. "Any paper 'round here?"

"You push the button." I did, and the heated wind blew.

"Was wondering what people did."

"You Mennonites?"

"No, we'se Amish folk."

Not to be confused, I knew, with Amana colonists, who lived nearby.

"Goin' ter wedding up at Riceville. Me brother-in-law's people." A shy, deferential smile, for he felt like a rube in the sophisticated world of this bus station.

"Where do you come from?"

"Indiana."

"Been on the road long?"

Before he could answer, the old man (could he actually be only my age?) walked in, stared angrily at me, and muttered grumpily in Amish-German to his son. The two left quickly, the boy cowed. I well understood the father's concern regarding his two guileless sons loose in the world and talking to strangers. What a lot of careful consideration must have gone into preparing for the trip and for something seemingly so frivolous as a wedding.

Back in the waiting room I sat down near the Amish family and considered trying to converse with the father. His current farming methods probably resembled those I'd known in the thirties. With his billy-goat beard he looked remarkably like Grandfather, whom I dimly recall lying in his coffin in 1931, one of my earliest memories.

I was curious to know this man's impressions of what he'd seen along the road thus far. We were both strangers in Iowa, each of us coming from a distance of time as well as miles. How to begin? I felt sure he could talk a worldly line if he had to—and did with his local banker and veterinarian. I watched him sign a traveler's check, which the ticket seller cashed for him. He was busily calculating expenses thus far incurred and probably wouldn't take kindly to an interruption.

The mother sat in majestic composure, knowing nobody would dare approach her, sturdy suitcases and a couple of nondescript parcels tucked closely around her voluminous black skirt. She drew out a small black leather box and placed it on her knees. A cosmetic case? Yet surely this woman never wore cosmetics. She had the sallow complexion of some Germans (was it diet or genes?), halfway between suet and cooked pork. She closed the box abruptly without making use of its contents. Just checking perhaps. It might be the portable dispensary, with pills, salves, powders, or even condiments.

They carried their food with them in a leather pouch big enough for a bowling ball. Now the younger son began to feed, eating a flaky substance that looked like granola, hand to face in rapid movements, the grain dribbling onto his clothes, some of it sticking to his fuzzy chin. One seldom saw a face like his these days: animal innocence, a visage as blank as a field. The older brother also began to eat. They were like puppies or kittens and especially vulnerable now in the rites of nourishment.

Although it was sunny, both boys wore heavy rubbers, no doubt because they'd been told to. The half dozen other passengers in the depot studied these odd-looking people and seemed to allow them the freedom to be different in what I remember as a typically Iowan attitude. One lady felt so good about her broad-mindedness and understanding that she tried to engage the Amish mother in a smile. But the mother ducked behind her bonnet ruffle, cutting off spectators.

The family kept its enclosure through a language that sounded like Grandmother's Plattdeutsch, which she spoke when telling a joke—and in her last years used most of the time. The mother's wire-rim glasses reinforced her homely plainness and added to her power. She muttered briefly to her husband without a trace of deference. Beyond her orbit, no doubt, he assumed authority, dealing with difficult matters such as the bus driver or the baggage clerk. This wedding trip was probably of her doing, so she kept a tough stance with her husband in case of complaints.

The northbound bus arrived and it looked full. We lined up to have our tickets punched before boarding. The Amish hung back, peering through the depot windows as if they couldn't decide whether this was the right bus. I controlled an urge to look out for them and shepherd them onto the vehicle. What business was it of mine?

I found a seat near the front on the aisle and spread out in the space under the window seat with my long legs. I saw the Amish moving toward the bus at last, the father supervising the luggage loading. Quite a few suitcases, no doubt full of wedding presents. The accordion ticket the father presented was unfamiliar to the driver and a controversy ensued. Finally they all climbed in, but there were almost no seats left. This troubled the other passengers a bit but nobody moved. The mother sat a few rows behind me next to an elderly woman; the father, after some distressful barking to the boys, finally settled down in the back. I quickly moved over to the window seat and snagged the youngest Amish boy for my seatmate. Then we were off.

"Your brother said it's a marriage you're headed for?"

"Yah, we'se goin' ter wedding." Blushing, half-laughing.

"Quite a trip—from Indiana. When'd you leave?" I had to repeat it and could feel his pulsing brain waves as he translated from Amish to English.

"Yest'day mornin'!" He swung his head back and forth, looking at the busy Cedar Rapids downtown streets. Here it was much too interesting to talk.

Up close his face was adolescent-bad, with tufts of unsightly whiskers. It would take a few more years for him to muster a real Amish beard.

We halted at stop signs, lurched forward.

He pointed to the warning sign in front: DO NOT STAND IN AISLES WHILE BUS IS MOVING. Did it mean he couldn't go to the toilet in the rear if he had to? Should there be curves up ahead, he was afraid he might be carsick. Earlier, on the hills and turns near the Mississippi River, he'd felt pretty queasy but managed not to throw up.

I assured him he could leave his seat whenever he felt like it. "And give yourself plenty of time." I didn't want him whoopsing on me.

Next he tried to find a notice that prohibited him from something he might get into his head to do, breaking the law without knowing it. Shouldn't talk to the driver. Cigarette smoking allowed only in the last four rows. No cigars. "I'se wantin' to understand the signs here."

How German he was! And how I was reminded of my own upbringing.

Not only had he never ridden a bus before, he'd never been in an automobile, either. I countered by telling him that I hadn't boarded a Greyhound until I was sixteen and off to take college entrance examinations at Grinnell. "That's when I left the farm—or at least that was the beginning."

When I mentioned growing up on a homestead about a hundred miles to the west, he was neither surprised nor curious, since everyone he knew farmed. His father worked eighty acres, he said, and I guessed how: with a primitive harrow, disc, single-bottom plow, and a team of horses; handpicking the corn; gathering in the sheaves of oats and wheat in biblical fashion, by hand. He didn't think to tell me anything about this, for it all seemed too ordinary to mention. Said he hadn't slept much all night because he didn't want to miss anything—though he'd dropped off now and then, awakening when the bus rode through a town.

I watched how eagerly he studied every farm we passed, getting a sense of the layout, the number and kind of animals, the machinery. Was this good for his Amish innocence?

Now in October, combines worked the soybean and corn fields. He recognized what they were but had never examined one up close. I wondered if he craved an opportunity to operate a big machine, but didn't ask. If he were going to be corrupted and take to the modern world, I'd rather he did it on his own without my help. Then, too, the Iowa farmer's fascination with huge machinery had resulted in a lot of financial hardship in the past as land prices fell and notes came due. Field work that used to take two or three weeks could now be done in that many days; but the farmer, riding in air-conditioned comfort and removed from the heat and dust of harvest had sometimes paid too much in borrowed money for the privilege. The cost of all this sophisticated machinery was out of sync with the size of the farm being worked.

After a silence that threatened to continue, I said, "The farmers seem to be all out picking corn" and asked whether Amish cornhuskers wore gloves with an extra thumb to use when the first one wore out. As a child I'd been fascinated by those six-digit gloves—what men had hands to fit them?

"Pullin' corn, we take a glove with a hook. That's best."

Then he pointed to an abandoned windmill, expressing concern that so many windmills weren't in use and some were half falling down.

That's because electric motors pump water now, I informed him. But some farmers kept the windmill standing for ornamentation or to use as a TV tower for better reception. "Anyhow, much of the groundwater is spoiled. Poisoned."

He turned, incredulous. "Poisoned? How?"

"Insecticides, herbicides, fertilizers—and too much runoff from feed lots. All of it got into the water supply. It's no good for drinking anymore. Can't use it for livestock and not safe for people either."

Once during a visit home, tubular plastic waterpipes were being laid below the frost line, connecting our farm to a reliable source of clean water. The new, elaborate conduit system was described to me as an enterprise similar to rural electrification in the thirties, an analogy I found disturbingly inappropriate. No more worry about your well going dry, I was told. This piped water originated in limestone rock—underground streams that also fed the Great Lakes.

Since every Iowa town had a bulbous watertank on stilts, the name in six-foot letters (part of the booster spirit as well as for identification), it was good to know that local farmers could now proudly point to *their* watertank. But I didn't take much comfort from this view of it.

Our house well was forty feet deep, and even during the worst drought years of the thirties it didn't go dry. Cool draughts of water would gush out of the pump spout after I'd leapt a good deal upon the iron handle with all my weight. I remember the satisfaction of that essential resource coming forth in response to my efforts—water that was quite hard and full of minerals. Healthy water, my New York City dentist called it years later, claiming it was responsible for my excellent teeth.

Few surface wells anywhere in the region—or the Middle West—were now safe for drinking. When I first learned of this, I thought bottled water might be a solution, remembering how matter-of-factly my wife and I had ordered a spring-water service when we lived in Laguna Beach, California. But of course I was forgetting the principal use of water on a farm: for the livestock. A single milk cow might drink thirty gallons a day. Contaminated water could result in milk that wouldn't test out; the taint of residues might pass into the flesh of hogs and cattle and eventually to people.

"So . . . the water's bad," said the Amish boy beside me.

"And getting worse. You people are best off farming the old way, believe me."

He told me they fertilized by manuring their fields and resigned themselves to losing a percentage of the crop to corn borers, grasshoppers, and other scourges rather than apply chemicals. They cross-cultivated in order to control the weeds somewhat.

"Make more on the dairy than the crops, anyhow." They milked eight Holsteins at present. I thought of Uncle Jack's neighbor, Lorne Nilles, whose herd numbered fifty, though *he* felt he was a small operator.

By now the boy had lost his wary look and was talking to me as if we'd known each other for some time. "Back a while, we'se in trouble 'cause of the cans."

"The milk cans?"

He nodded. They'd been used to placing their cans on the roadside each morning for pickup. But local health authorities ruled that all milk sold commercially must be extracted from the cows by milking machines, then kept in refrigerated holding tanks. Some friend high in the Indiana bureaucracy had intervened on their behalf, however. "Otherwise, don't know what we'd a done!" Mechanical milkers ran counter to their religious beliefs.

A few miles farther on we spotted our first horse. "That one's obviously for riding," I said, adding that I'd never handled a team on our farm, though we had two nags out to pasture that were harnessed up in threshing season to pull the grain wagons.

"Treat a horse right, he'll work for years. Won't wear out like a machine." A sanctimonious smile.

Some farmers on small acreages in the East and South, I said, were using horses instead of tractors on marginal land—especially organic farmers and those concerned about ecology. He didn't know what I was talking about, though it worried him that the price for horses might be driven up because of these enthusiasts.

When we arrived in Vinton, I crawled out of my seat to fetch a road map from my bag stowed overhead.

Indiana—here; now what town did you say you're from?

He pointed, face aglow. *Paoli.* Not far from Louisville, Kentucky, and way south of Bloomington, Indiana. They had begun the journey from the depot at Redmond's Cafe in Paoli. He spotted the village names on the map as if recognizing old friends. All within horse-driving buggy range: French Lick, Becks Mill, Livonia, Leipsic, Orleans, Ethel, and Valeena.

Approaching Waterloo, we drove by an enormous road construction project, the concrete pylons already installed. "What's all this? Who's payin' for it?" he asked. Earth-moving vehicles had piled the rich, black, river-bottom soil into what looked like slag heaps.

"Taxpayers. It's another road. Digging up and throwing away good Iowa soil just so drivers can go a little faster."

He, too, thought it crazy that this four-laner wasn't enough—that it must be enlarged to six or eight. I ranted and raved a little. All this land for interstates, all across the country, removed from crop production; why, it was big enough when you added it all up to feed a good portion of Africa.

"People always want more, seems like. Never satisfied, what they got." Though he was. He set his mouth firmly, just like his father.

Waterloo, a few minutes later, was a rest stop, and the depot was smoky and crowded. The two boys told me they were thirsty and went to hunt for a water fountain. There was none. The ticket seller directed them to the restaurant next door. I followed because I figured they might run into trouble ordering only a glass of water.

We found the cafe full of customers. I noticed water in glasses on trays, ready to be passed around by the waitresses, so I simply handed a glass to each of the youths. Nobody paid us any attention or asked if we'd like to be seated. The boys were shocked by my bold action but pleased—stealing water! Defying the rules!

We returned to the bus, where the Amish parents remained, the only passengers not availing themselves of the rest stop. The youngsters informed their parents where water was to be found and the mother requested some, too. This time the youngest went in alone with a devilish look on his face and came back with a styrofoam cup. "They'se afraid I'd take the glass," he said to me knowingly. He handed her the water as if she were ailing—gently and reverently.

Later when everyone was again on board, I asked my seatmate if his mother was in poor health. "Oh no, she's fine. Can hardly wait to get to the weddin'."

The location of Riceville puzzled me; I asked where it was exactly. The man across the aisle piped up and said it lay close to the Minnesota border; his companion mentioned nearby towns. Obviously they'd been listening to us all along. We drew out the maps again and I finally found Riceville.

"Quite a distance from here. Is somebody meeting you?"

"Yeah, supposed to."

They would disembark at Cedar Falls just ahead—as I would too. Now with evening coming on, could a horse and carriage make the journey to Riceville? Wouldn't it be dangerous for them to be on the roads in a buggy with only a dinky lantern hanging out back for a taillight?

No time to ask these questions; we were arriving. "I enjoyed the talk! Hope you have a great time at the wedding."

"I'se sure gonna try."

"And if I were you I'd stay . . . I mean, stay where you are. On the farm. It's a good life, isn't it? You don't have to see the whole country to know that."

My remark puzzled him. I'd said too much of course. What I'd

meant was that he didn't seem a likely candidate to climb out of
where he was, so he shouldn't make himself miserable trying.

I reached down for the briefcase under my legs. "I'm speaking
here tonight—at the university."

Blank face. Or was it that he'd been taught to tune out all that
was alien or might endanger his views and throw him off course?
Because I'd once been as innocent—almost—as this kid, I couldn't
stop myself from trying to awaken him a little. After all, how
disconcerting would it be for him to know that the world exists in
other forms? I drew out a few of my books. "I wrote these," and
pointed to my name.

He was not impressed. No interest or curiosity, just the
expressionless look. Either his father had schooled him well or the
remoteness of his life protected him from the likes of me. Perhaps it
had been vain of me to try to dazzle this kid; *that* might have been all
I was doing.

Then the father's hand fell heavily on his shoulder. In a jabber
of scolding Amish-German, the boy was drawn out of his seat as if
by a rope and hauled to the rear, where his family pulled down
parcels in readiness to leave. I saw the old guy's fierce, authoritarian
face mellowing to smugness now that he had his sons back close
beside him. No more prattle, no suggestion of choices, no divergence
from ecclesiastical laws and family rules. Years ago I outdistanced
the grasp of men like him, and I was glad to be living beyond the
strictures of the old-ways generation. I must remember that.

The bus driver announced over the speaking system that we were
five minutes ahead of schedule. Looking out the window, I saw
nobody at the depot waiting to meet me—which didn't entirely
surprise me. I knew how these university engagements often went.

I stepped down from the bus ahead of the Amish family, but the
boy who'd been my seatmate caught up with me, hand extended. "So
long, mister!"

We shook hands heartily. "When is that wedding? Not tonight,
I hope."

"Tomorrow. They got me waitin' on tables with two girls."

"Who *are* these girls?"

He giggled, blushing. "I'se supposed to get to know 'em."

For purposes of healthy crossbreeding; that's why he was
blushing.

Awhile back I'd asked how many Amish resided in his community and after some quiet calculation, plus a bit of finger counting, he'd come up with twenty families all told. His sister had married an Iowa Amish man; now a girl among them would be found for this boy as well as for his brother. A serious trip indeed! Tomorrow's wedding would bring together all the Amish of northeast Iowa, a good chance for the young to look each other over and make their choices. Keep them down on the farm that way.

"Will your visit last long?"

"Don't know . . . maybe go home next week." With a bashful smile he added, "Or could stay."

Depended, obviously, on how well he got on with his courting. At that moment I noticed his father placing their suitcases and bundles in the trunk of a big black Cadillac that had just pulled up. "What's this? No horse and buggy?"

"We'se got to get there."

The driver, wearing a homespun suit with no buttons, was clearly Amish. "But I thought cars weren't allowed."

His mother overheard and gave me a sharp look but said nothing, just moved over to the hood of the gleaming Cadillac and set her traveling case on it. After unlatching the lid, she took off the poke bonnet and let her auburn hair fall in maidenlike waves over her shoulders. The two boys, still wearing rubbers, opened the rear car door and climbed into the crimson plush interior, swallowed up in the Amish world by this unlikely means. The mother began brushing her hair, stroke after stroke. She glanced at me with almost a smile, as if to say, What makes you think you know anything about us?

Next day I am home on the farm, close again to all that held me tightly when young and from which I was determined to escape—and have for the most part. By living a very different, largely urban life, I manage to keep the past distinct from the present. A necessary maneuver perhaps. Nobody can repossess childhood—or should want to, too much—but I feel lucky that I'm able to visit the exact place on earth where for me all the beginnings happened.

I prefer to arrive in early fall when the nights are crisp, the days blue and gold, and the question "How're the crops this year?" has largely been answered.

Ownership of worked land holds people in one place longer than might otherwise be true. There are hundreds in the home region I'm acquainted with. Relatives and neighbors will have me in for meals, setting full tables; mostly homegrown food, from the roast beef (well done) to the potatoes and cherry pie. I'll observe the differences since the last time: how the young have grown, the old aged; hear who got married; learn of births, deaths, good fortune and disaster. Like counting the rings on the stump of a felled tree, I'll determine how much margin to allot the past year.

Nobody will find it odd that I should be interested in keeping up these primal connections, since for one thing, I still own a piece of the farm. My presence is understandable because of business reasons. I'll be asked, "Where're you at now?" or "Not teaching anymore? What sort of work, then?"

I know the profession of writing is not considered a job, so it is easiest to explain that I run Yaddo, an arts organization in Saratoga Springs, New York, where writers, visual artists, and composers reside for a month or two. The statement sounds so strange that there is usually no follow-up. With these preliminaries over, it'll be possible for me to find out about *them* and myself in relation to them, which is why I've come.

Uncle Jack, born in this house in 1896 and having lived here most of the years since, spends little time on memories. Too much of that sort of thing he feels "could get a fella down." Once I remember him shaking his head with a smile upon my arrival, saying, "You've no idea how quiet it gets around here!"

Of course he no longer inhabits the exact world *I* knew here as a child. For instance, the strict rules prescribed by Grandfather and continued in the family have largely disappeared. Uncle Jack even keeps a bottle of peppermint schnapps in the pantry to serve visiting neighbors. He socializes with Catholics and enjoys the company of a priest at local basketball games, not feeling the gulf between Lutherans and Catholics, which used to be such a divisive feature of local life.

The furnishings of the house do not speak to Uncle Jack from the past, as they do for me, because he has carried them along with him into the present. I look at the oak dining room chairs clustered around the table; at the handpainted china in the glass-front cupboard, dishes my aunts fired in the basement kiln during the years before World War I; a Felix the cat doorstop done with a jigsaw by cousin Don in grade school; and my own varnished plywood magazine rack, constructed for Mother, a great reader—a project in seventh-grade manual training class. All of these objects seem to spark connections between what's not here as well. This setting has endured for a long time now, and I am preparing for the end of it.

I couldn't have a better guide for the transition than Uncle Jack, the youngest of six who grew up in this house at the turn of the century. When he and my father married sisters, they set up housekeeping under this roof, and I'm the sixth of seven who were of the next generation.

After such a tumult of people, how strange that the only resident now was one octogenarian who had never been all that keen about farming in the first place. On my last visit Uncle Jack had just survived a bout of pneumonia, which brought him near death from uremic poisoning. His legs were still ulcerating and he was forced to keep them propped up for more time than he cared to spend in such a supine position. The ailment brought to mind two of his dead sisters, who also suffered from circulatory problems. "Our family gets it in the legs. That's our weak spot," he said to me by way of warning.

While on the subject of family ailments, I ask about his oldest sister Mary, who died in 1915, twelve years before I came along.

She suffered from dropsy, nowadays we'd call it leukemia, he says.

I don't question that diagnosis but know he's wrong. Of the four girls, she was the first to hold a job, taking a position as a teacher and assistant principal in the local public school. During that time she continued living on the farm, though later she taught in Sioux City. She died in her early thirties after years of poor health.

He frowns, shakes his head. "My sisters, all of 'em so good in school—do you think they'd pay any attention to a fella? Help me with my studies?"

He couldn't understand arithmetic, and although everyone at home knew Johnny was having trouble with his schoolwork, nobody took the time to sit down and try to help him. Later it always rankled that he hadn't managed to finish eighth grade. Yet Jack seemed to me reliable enough in doing sums and simple calculations; he even served as secretary of the farmers' elevator and was often treasurer of the church. ("They know they can trust me," he'd say with a laugh.) I think his resentment stemmed from the fact that without math and a decent education, he had been disqualified from an engineering career, the field where his talents lay. What might he have accomplished if he'd just had the chance!

Uncle Jack glanced now at the booming television set in the corner—a convenient way to stop talk or change the subject. I sensed he was ashamed of this video time wasting. He would rather be out in the toolshop making something on the lathe. He was embarked upon a project to recreate scaled-down metal models of all the tractors he'd ever owned, each model to be powered in some way or partially mobile. Similarly, when his sister Elizabeth retired from teaching, she set a goal of doing needlepoint staircase risers depicting each of the houses she'd lived in—to be installed on the steps of her parents' 1920s retirement house (which she'd inherited) in the nearby town of Remsen. Neither of them would finish these enterprises, but I recognized the commitment to keep going that such visions induced.

"*Ach,* it does no good thinking about things too much," he often said to me, roughly covering an emotional moment. Perhaps we had happened upon mention of his sons' deaths; or the strokes and fatal illness of his wife, Lizzie; or the death of his brother and farm business partner, my father, in 1928—an event which put Jack in the role of being responsible for everyone in this house.

In the deep night hours the silence is so enormous that I revel in the gift of aural nothingness after the constant hum and crash of New York City night sounds. On my visit one year the raccoons were stripping Juneberries from the bushes near the back door, making such a racket with their squealing and quarreling that I had to shout out the window to silence them. Uncle Jack snored peacefully through it all—as *I* had slept through the fire sirens when he visited me in New York, though he had been kept awake by them much of the night.

Here on the farm the night dark is astonishingly complete. Even in Saratoga Springs, where I live over half the time, the lights of Albany diffuse the blackness. I'm a participant in the total evening darkness on the farm, though I don't know exactly in how many ways. Such a thorough fade-out suggests illumination to come. Is it that I hope to discover why I don't live where I was born? Most people never bother to ask themselves that question, for in America the need to move on seems allied with the business of growing up.

Occasionally I speculate on what it would be like to resettle on the homeplace some day; such an existence, particularly in old age, might seem to round out life nicely. But my good sense tells me there would be nothing I could do connected with farming even if I owned the whole place. I never took to agriculture as a kid, am fairly inept with machines, and am no good at handling tools. Most things mechanical baffle me, and although I enjoy simple gardening, I have little of the dexterity essential for a modern farmer.

In China, parts of Europe, the Middle East, and other areas of the world where I've lived or visited, one's native village and location of birth is a lifelong special pact, sometimes a holy bond. But in the United States we subscribe to the notion that one can abandon the place where consciousness dawned, the wind was first felt, the sun known—where one was nourished by the warmth of family flesh close by.

Gertrude Stein once said, "Americans are the most abstract of people," and I take her to mean that we have the ability to separate ourselves from essential life connections almost at will. Adept at pulling up stakes, settling anew, becoming someone else with different speech, appearance, and no baggage of personal history anywhere in evidence.

But I'm sure we never can be, in most respects, anybody other than we always were from the very beginning. I'm one of the lucky individuals with an actual home setting still to be connected to, though I don't literally believe ancestors hang about the eaves of the farmhouse or ghosts stalk the bedrooms. For me, associations thicken the very air, inside and out, even in the barns, where I remember long-gone animals—horses, pigs, cows—beings I once knew intimately, whose distinct personalities I sensed.

It's not necessary to bury yesterday in order to justify one's present. I'm always keen to discover what is new here in my old stamping grounds. Uncle Jack used to be especially interested in showing me what progress had been made in contour farming, biodegradable pest controls, modern milch herd equipment, and gadgetry on farm machinery. My past has an overlay of the present—of which I'll never be a part.

Recently a tornado swerved through the farm, demolishing part of the one-hundred-year-old grove, missing the house but badly damaging the large shed where Jack stored machinery and worked on his inventions. In the aftermath he resolutely reset the sill on its foundation with a tractor-lift. When I remarked to him once, "You're lucky the twister didn't destroy the house," he replied, "That's what people keep telling me, but frankly, I'd rather have the grove."

The house, now that he was left alone with its contents of three generations, obviously seemed a burden. Although I am well into middle age, my soft old overalls, jackets, and shirts—most of which still fit me—hang in the closet of "the boy's room." I look at these objects—plus roller skates, an old tennis racket, several golf clubs, and a silverfoil, homemade badminton trophy for which we kids keenly contested some summer of the 1930s—and instead of feeling melancholy, the connection to years long gone elates me. Familiar objects of childhood don't deny the passage of time, only disarm the finality of it. Presumably if one had the patience and desire, the lost moments could be purled back into existence. But there's no need to when the evidence of the possibility to do so is clear.

I'm aware that the time approaches, perhaps quite soon, when the homeplace will be occupied by strangers. "If something should happen to me . . . " Jack would preface offhand advice about farm management, indicating where he kept his records and who could be called upon for help. But he refused to take that prudent but difficult extra step of giving away his farm in acreage parcels each year to his daughter and grandsons in order to avoid the huge inheritance tax that would burden them. It might even become necessary upon his passing for the farm to be sold just to pay the tax liabilities. And although Jack vaguely realizes that, he cannot act.

The house might be torn down if the farm were sold; the grove uprooted in order to enlarge the cornfields. Should that happen, it probably would no longer make such a crucial difference to me, for if ever I neared this sacred spot of soil, something would still tell me where I was: back at the center once again.

MINING THE FAMILY LODE

It's happening: the white china kitchen doorknob is in my adult hand where my child fingers once reached. I am pushing the door in to the same sound of squeaking hinges. To the left is the crank-handle wall phone, black tulip mouthpiece mute to the conversations of decades. It remains hanging there as part of the furnishings, though long ago the line was connected to a dial phone.

To walk into a complete, almost exact setting of one's childhood rooms can be like probing a sore: the itching breeds more pain than relief but one can't stop scratching. I've set myself up as being strong enough to take this without flinching or wallowing in sentiment.

What causes this aching rawness? Not just loved ones missed. It's closer to the bone than that—a mourning for one's own lost years. Here I'm coming around the corner right into it instead of experiencing the gradual time accumulation, a receding away, each year from the next.

All of us were so alive here once; now the house is a passive monument to that activity.

In the dining room Uncle Jack has made a nest for himself in an easy chair within range of the TV control, newspapers, medicines, tissue box, fruit bowl, and other comforts. His bedroom and bathroom are nearby. I note a large laundry basket where all his soiled clothes and bed linens are tossed—for some woman to take care of. (It'll be his daughter, Lois, who periodically makes the forty-mile trip from her husband's farm.) Dust and cobwebs all over the place, but Uncle Jack doesn't want a cleaning woman to come in and perhaps question his arrangements—some outsider he'd have "to deal with," who might report on him to everybody. Blind in one eye, the other magnified behind a thick lens, he doesn't see any dirt. He knows I won't interfere or intimate cleaner standards by getting out the vacuum cleaner. No, I'll let it all be. He'll fix fried eggs, coffee, and toast for me each morning, enjoying his role of once again taking care of "one of the kids."

Uncle Jack cherishes his independence, and so long as he can keep his restricted driver's license, life can be maintained as it is. But I'm concerned when he tells me how little peripheral vision he actually has, that he drives the two and a half miles to Remsen for "dinner," the hot noonday meal in Ruth's Cafe, by lining up the car fender with the weedy edge of the highway and going very, very slowly.

In the house of Florence and Lorne Nilles, his neighbors and renters, he partakes of many meals and romps with their small children. He has worked out a good old age for himself and doesn't want to lose it until the last possible moment. But his muscles and body movements are no longer to be trusted; his reflexes play tricks.

Out in the grove he enjoys operating his homemade sawmill, slicing out planks from our trees naturally felled in storms. Neighbors sometimes haul logs over for him to cut, particularly their valuable timber like black walnut. One day he missed his footing, fell to the ground, and the tractor ran over him, barreling straight ahead, grinding itself into the fir trees until it finally choked and gave up. He managed to get to his feet and slowly made his way to the house, where he telephoned Florence Nilles: "Say . . . are you busy?"

No, why?

"Could you come over here once?"

Is something the matter, Jack?

"The tractor ran over me and I better get to the hospital."

The doctor who examined him found, miraculously, that there were no broken bones, though his back and legs were severely bruised. "What's an old fellow like you doing on a tractor anyhow?" the doctor scolded. To which Jack, irritated, replied: "It's old fellows like me who pay the doctor's bills and keep him in business."

Since my last visit, Uncle Jack's annual physical exam revealed cancer in the colon. Surgery took place at once. He got through it successfully, but his daughter Lois told me on the phone that the doctor thought the malignancy had spread, perhaps to the liver. Very likely it was "only a matter of time."

Jack wasn't informed of this dire prognosis. Much to everyone's surprise he kept on with his life very well, undertaking chemotherapy with considerable interest because of its scientific aspects. This new thing had happened—something rather important, at least to him. He sought to learn what he could about cancer of this type not so much because he was determined to cure himself (he left that to the doctors) but out of sheer curiosity, because it was what he had. He'd heard so much about marijuana smoking—and that medical uses for it were allowed to counter sensations of nausea from chemotherapy. Now might be the time to try it. But when he asked, the doctor informed him: "Where you had cancer, the marijuana smoke wouldn't reach that far." Jack laughed, telling me. Was he perhaps wondering if I—being from big New York City after all—had access to a supply? No, I didn't think so. Just curious and open to possibilities.

The Nilleses drove Jack to his regular therapy sessions, where patients in a group received instructions on how to get along with their illnesses. He was eager to attend, just as he might want to take a class in metalworking, electronics, or any other area of practical information and knowledge which it might be good to investigate.

In church, friends asked him solicitously: "How *are* you?" to which he'd reply frankly with a directness they couldn't handle, "Oh, I had an operation for cancer, you know. I'm on chemotherapy now, and it sure takes the starch out of you." Such a strange look would come into their eyes when he said right out that he had cancer—he reported to me—but he didn't care. "If they don't want to shake my hand or turn away, so what? People are funny." Before long, he added, not many were asking him how he was.

Uncle Jack prefers to view my visit now as a side trip from my regular business travels, not a possible last call. He figures I'll want to see friends from early days at school, catch up on the news. But too much has happened in these parts since I left. It's the past that holds the most promise for me, although I sense difficulties getting into it. Yes, here I am in the familiar rooms of the house, but the enclosures feel vaguely content-less, like the termite-hollowed shells of walls that still stand but are without substance. Everything important here I seem to be bringing with me, in my own head.

Jack is the last spokesman who can reach as far back in time as I'm interested in going—way before my years, to the point where he is reaching behind his own. I nudge up against questions without knowing how to ask them. Sometimes he speaks endlessly about current happenings that don't interest me much. I wait patiently for a chance to divert the narrative stream into more productive channels.

"Let's get out those photo albums once," Jack says, moving slowly to the closed double doors of the parlor, behind which he stashed all of the undistributed belongings from his sister's house, which he inherited a few years before when Elizabeth died. Jack would be spending the rest of his life in occasional half-hearted attempts to make piles for each of us in that room of memorabilia and family artifacts. I called it "the treasure room," but that was before I realized what still lay in the attic for my discovery.

Now he hauls out a photobook devoted to Grandmother Louisa's sisters, brothers, and parents. No identification under any of the posed studio portraits, but Jack recognizes who they are from childhood acquaintance. I write the names down in pencil so as not to disturb the pristine matte surface: Greimans who once lived (and many descendants still do) in the region around Mason City, Iowa, their offspring numbering many hundreds by now. But for whom am I making this careful recording? I have no children to pass any of it on to.

"That's Herman—Ma's youngest brother."

A handsome youth with a somewhat rakish look in his eye. I didn't recall meeting any of his progeny at those enormous Greiman family reunions we used to have in state parks in the thirties and forties. In fact, I didn't remember hearing of this Herman before.

"No, you wouldn't have. He went West."

"Oh?" I could tell by Jack's embarrassed, sideway look that there was some anecdote here.

"Herman kind of got next to a woman . . . and she had a baby."

"So what happened?"

The woman sued and the court awarded her Herman's eighty acres, his stake back there in eastern Iowa. "Never learned why he didn't marry her." Anyhow, Herman moved away, traveled by train to Remsen, stopping over to visit with his sister. Then on to Montana, where he homesteaded and lived the rest of his life. "Sure, you've got relatives in Montana, but we don't know who they are, where they might be living. Uncle Herman wasn't much for writing to the family—not after what happened."

Montana. Aunts Bertha and Elizabeth, on one of their many summer motor excursions, drove to Montana specifically to look up their cousins. For years afterward, Christmas cards and birthday greetings were exchanged and funeral telegrams when necessary. But I say nothing about this recollection to Jack, who seems to have forgotten more about the family than I have. Of course, it could be I'm entirely wrong. I recall hearing of an Elmer, a cousin of Grandpa's who lived in Montana, and my aunts may have been visiting him, not Herman's offspring.

I haven't been watching the time, and now it's nearly noon. Although I'd risen late and eaten a big breakfast (more substantial fare than I'm used to), Jack says that unless we get to Ruth's Cafe right away, we might not be able to sit in his usual booth. Also, some of the specials on the menu will probably be gone.

Since we're mining a good vein of the family lode, I'm loath to stop. At the restaurant there'll be cronies and acquaintances; it'll be hard to keep a continuity of this kind of talk. But he wants to leave.

I do the driving and upon arrival he greets the regulars with a wave of his hand toward me: "All the way from New York City." I nod and smile, for they all know who I am, though I can't place them right off. We order bowls of chickeny rice soup, beef stew with noodles, and steam-blanched beans; but the meal begins with the inevitable cup of coffee, "regular."

Jack is now going over favorite Army tales (mention of New York must have prompted him): how he'd served in the fire department at Camp Mills, Long Island, in 1918. I've heard these stories dozens of times and by now I'm not much interested in them. But I pick up on his meditative comment, "The war changed everything for me."

"How so?"

When his girlfriend, Lizzie, journeyed to Long Island to visit him, he became aware of her difficult home situation. Her father and stepmother had decided to move from the farm and retire to a small house in Remsen where, alas, there would be no room for her. "Lizzie kind of got left out." She didn't fancy being a girl-helper elsewhere, however. She had little education or training and no prospects; what should she do? The other daughters of the house, my mother and the stepsisters, were either teaching school or had already married and lived away. "Well, there probably would have been a bed for her to sleep in, but nothing to occupy her much. On a farm it's different."

An older stepsister, Mabel, who by now had several children and

GRANDPARENTS LOUISA AND JOHN HARNACK, 1892,
WITH INFANT HENRY, WHO WOULD BECOME MY FATHER.

needed help to cope with her farmhouse work, took Lizzie in for a time. Years later this kindness was reciprocated when Mabel's children boarded with us in order to ride along in our Model A Ford to the best high school, in the county seat town.

But Lizzie's move to Mabel's was only temporary, not a solution to her problem. I gather from Jack's remarks that she put her situation to him plainly while visiting him at Camp Mills. And he was deeply affected by her sad tale. Both of them had felt the web of family obligations—at the mercy of other people's plans, which impinged upon their lives. But if the two of them stuck together—yes, it might all be different. The war emergency forced them to attempt to secure a piece of personal destiny for themselves; they would have some of the life owed them. And how lucky that they realized they were much the same sort, would do well as a pair.

Financially, how would they manage? Getting away from grueling farm labor had been a big factor behind Jack's enlistment. In any case, for the moment they could do nothing; he still might be shipped overseas and now was no time to start a marriage. Months later at his severing out, he received a job offer from the fire department of New York City. In after years he often wondered, what if he'd taken them up on it? But upon discharge he returned home to the farm, with the aim of marrying soon.

He participated in a lottery open only to ex-servicemen for free government land available in Wyoming. Didn't win. But if he had, would he have been saved from a too early marriage? No, I gather that wasn't the issue. "The different ones in Lizzie's family were pretty surprised to hear she might be going with me to Wyoming." Nobody had expected her rescue to be quite so romantically spectacular.

My father and mother's marriage in 1920 probably determined the actual course of events for Jack and Lizzie. In accordance with custom, the older generation must make room for the younger. Therefore, "Pa" and "Ma" would retire to Remsen with unmarried Bertha, while Henry and his bride (and soon Jack and Lizzie) would have the farm.

Construction of a modern stucco house in town began. A carload of bricks arrived from Greiman country in eastern Iowa, paid for with money Grandpa kept in a bank run by his nephew Arthur (after whom I received my middle name because he was

MOTHER AND LIZZIE (second and third from the left)
WITH THEIR STEPSISTERS AND STEPBROTHERS, C. 1915.

(From left) LIZZIE, STEPSISTER MABEL, AND MOTHER
ON A PILE OF CORN, THE LANG FARM, C. 1910.

Father's closest friend). In addition to family loyalty, the reason Grandpa's funds were there was that the bank paid 1 percent more interest than others. A good thing Grandpa got his money out in bricks, we often heard later, for the bank went bust early in the Depression.

Grandpa took an active, professional interest in the house construction, he and his sons doing most of the carpentry, and Lizzie cooked meals and helped in the moving. Her sterling qualities became apparent to Grandpa. A solid, hard-working woman, surely a good prospective wife for young Johnny, who needed settling down a bit. "For the first time with me, Dad wasn't so severe and critical all the time. Seemed friendlier, you know?" Always before there had been that element of strain and parental disapproval. Now the old man thought better of his son for having snared such a fine fiancée. "So it was Lizzie who brought a sort of peace between us."

Jack is almost making a story of it for me, doing my literary job. Or is it that the venerable father-and-son tale is remarkably persistent and we are getting to the heart of a business that often requires the turning of years—and more glowing attention than one alone can give. Sixty years brooding over it, but here's a son coming at last to terms with his father, the tale still raw in the telling, a wound that's painful whenever he thinks about it. Maybe Jack senses that in different ways we're both seeking to understand the dead and the ever-living past.

"About my father . . . " I begin, and he looks up sharply. The waitress interrupts, swinging a Silex, and our cups are filled for a third time while Jack joshes with her. When we're alone again, I continue: "I was wondering . . . he went to high school, I know, but did he hope to go to college?"

"Hank never made it through high school."

"But I thought . . . That's what Mother used to say."

"*She* was educated—college even—but Hank never graduated from high school. Only went in winter, the way they did in those days. For farmers it was the only time you could go to school."

There's a neutral tone to this discussion; he realizes I never knew my father, who died six months after I was born. Even now I feel rather impersonal asking these questions; it isn't the book version of how it's supposed to be. Just being curious rather than emotional about it. Since my mother and her brood of four remained in Uncle

MY MOTHER AND FATHER'S WEDDING PICTURES, 1920.

(From left) MOTHER, FATHER WITH INFANT ROBERT,
JACK, LIZZIE, GRANDMA, GRANDPA, 1921.
JACK PITCHED BALL FOR THE TOWN OF STRUBLE.

Jack's household, the dead father's missing-ness was played down. For my older brothers it must have been different, but I never felt a need for the father search. Here was Uncle Jack and he was enough. Now I'm asking questions mostly because doctors often query about one's family health history, and Father's death at thirty-six is always a red flag.

How did he die? I never heard a clear, reliable story from anyone. Was it pneumonia or heart trouble or a little of both? The obituary reference in the local paper, which I'd once come across, was solemnly vague. In the photo albums he didn't appear to be physically robust, like Jack; had a rather small head and thin neck for his somewhat rangy frame. Once while exploring Mother's trunk in the attic I found a few of his legendary twenty-dollar dress shirts, tried them on, and although they were too tight under the arms and a couple inches short in the sleeves, I could wear them in summer, the cuffs rolled up.

Still do. That Henry allowed himself these luxuries was one of the few personality factors I knew about him. He definitely liked clothes. I see him photographed in a belted, Norfolk jacket, which doesn't fit too well—but he certainly makes a dashing impression. In another snapshot he stands grinning, very much of the lively twenties, in an ankle-length fur coat. Perhaps needed for winter warmth, but still a bit rakish for an Iowa farmer.

He and Mother had gotten a rather late start in marriage for those years, he twenty-eight and she thirty. They had us four children in seven years; then he was dead.

Uncle Jack now tells me that Henry's health had been poor long before he married and took on the farm and family responsibilities.

Just what was wrong?

"Bad tonsils. They were taken out by a Sioux City surgeon who botched the job."

How so?

"They grew back, kind of closing up his throat so he couldn't breathe."

The local doctor sent him to the Mayo Clinic in Rochester, Minnesota, where "they skinned his whole throat."

The year? It was 1915 or 1916, either before or after their sister Mary died.

Economically, those were the best agricultural times. Grand-

MY FATHER IN THE EARLY 1920s.

father suddenly became rather affluent, along with most other thrifty, hardworking farmers in northwest Iowa lucky enough to have stuck it out on this good land through the difficult pioneering period. With his prize herd of Black Angus, some of them registered, and crops bringing premium prices—no taxes to speak of—Grandfather could afford to give his daughters a life of culture, education, and travel of a sort he and his wife had never known. And pay for whatever treatment might be necessary for his ailing son, Henry.

"I remember Hank was sick the same year Aunt Mary died," Jack said. This was the Mary who was Grandfather's sister; she was married to Jack's Uncle Adolph. "And later that winter, Hank and Uncle Adolph went down to Hot Springs, Arkansas—for the baths."

How European of them to take themselves off to a spa for a cure, the one suffering emotionally, the other physically. "They stayed in Hot Springs all winter?"

Yes, playing the horses at night, taking the waters during the day, indulging in a little gambling. "It seemed to do them both good."

Just as we are deep in these family matters, a woman I don't remember having seen before comes up to our table, calls me by my first name, and says: "Oh Jack, are you telling him stories again?"

He looks sheepish, blushes, and shuts up. After she's gone he tells me who she is—a distant relative, actually (most people around here seem to be), but he doesn't care to speak further about intimate family concerns; everybody seems to be watching us. I realize with disappointment that it'll be hours or days before we might drift back to these meaty subjects in a natural way.

Before leaving the cafe, Jack uses a phrase "have a horse on you" which I pick up on at once. Exactly what does it mean?

When you shake dice to determine who is to pay for the coffee, the first-round winner says, "I've got a horse on you," and then the other one rolls. If the "down" opponent wins that time, he says: "Now I've got a horse on *you.*" A third shake determines who triumphs. I recall seeing the black rubber cup near the cash register in bars and restaurants, remember the jolly talk and bantering. Vaguely sinful gambling of a sort we Lutherans weren't supposed to indulge in.

As we stroll out to the street, Jack informs me I'm not the only visitor who's come back recently to prowl around. Two second cousins on my mother's side spent several days making a pilgrimage to each of the homesteads where their grandfathers and great-uncles had once lived. After years of teaching school in separate locations (one widowed, the other never married), they now lived together, and genealogical pursuits focused their days. In the ladders of carefully constructed family connections they busily worked their way back through the centuries and around the globe in reverse from the original westward migration to small villages in northern Germany, Denmark, and Switzerland.

These schoolteachers didn't notify the people who now owned or rented the farms in question to tell them they planned an inspection. They just showed up, in typical country fashion. Who would have the nerve to go into it on the telephone? You did it in person if you did it at all. They explained cavalierly who they were and why they were interested in looking around the place. Scrutinized the barns and outbuildings, requested permission to enter the houses. Yes, they were allowed in everywhere, these old ladies on such a sentimental mission.

The more Jack talked about them, the better I remembered those two. Now I'm wondering why they did it—and is *my* business here much the same? What were they looking for?

How times change! Yes, but here in rural northwest Iowa not as fast as in other areas. In a locality where farming is still the prime factor in almost everyone's life, the long hold of the pioneer experience continues its grip. I am of a generation that still felt the clan's nurturing power, witnessed the banding together in times of trouble—everyone helping as needed—the way it was done during those hard years of settling on the prairie. Your relatives were your best friends; blood could be counted on—the ultimate safeguard.

Now those of us who remember that primal bonding have reached middle or old age, with time on our hands. Libraries contain new reference books on how to trace ancestors. It becomes a great plot to follow, a story to unravel. And there's literally no end to how far you can go, traveling to the archives of state historical societies and getting in touch with the Mormons, who have computerized holdings of family names. The rest of America may have forgotten the feel of life in a large family, but we will continue to sense the warmth in a reflected way by taking up the search for "roots."

Yes, it's something to do, but more: It helps alleviate the awful chill of contemporary life, which is generally devoid of family layerings. Nowadays you don't go to relatives if you're in trouble; you're usually better off with good, understanding friends. But as you age and "your time" nears, the family comes forward in a more real way. You want to find that family even if most of them are spirits by now, gone away or "passed over."

I understand how my two elderly cousins had "gotten a horse on" the past merely by looking around on the farmsteads of the preceding generations. Just when modern life of the last half century has cleared the way for an escape from the obligations and duties of family bonds, when we no longer have to think about caring for the old or the ones who can't quite make it and rush away from the perceived awfulness of the tight family into the great freedom of permissive contemporary life, some individuals turn around and try to get back into the snugness and security that the family enclosure once gave. Nobody can climb back in that way. But the passionate genealogists, infirm of limb and heedless of consequences—aware that the younger generations aren't much interested—still seek the revelations of research. And one day when these youngsters are feeling too much alone in the world, they'll have a place to go, something to hang onto. Then they will discover the rest of us. Who have always been here.

CALLED BACK

The next time I returned, Uncle Jack was approaching his eighty-fifth birthday; he seemed much thinner and shorter. I recalled the big man he had been most of his life, six feet tall and weighing 220 pounds or more. Now in addition to his gaunt physique, he had lost that inner vitality and optimism which kept him young and up to the minute, a keen witness and participant of the day.

He suffered from bone cancer and was in considerable pain when the medication "didn't take"; there were more ulcerating sores on his legs. To pass the time he half-watched kiddie cartoons on TV

JACK, IN HIS WORLD WAR I ARMY UNIFORM,
WITH HENRY AND ANNA, 1917.

but from a great distance. Normally he would be out in the machine shop, but now after breakfast he spent hours close to the bathroom. The period indoors forced him to consider his present state, and he didn't like what he knew but was unflinching in the face of it. While I was home perhaps for the final time, what needed to be done had to be done; things still to say must be said.

Business first. Jack had always acted as agent for the eighty acres my siblings and I owned. Land-renting arrangements could be put in the hands of a man at the local bank, for instance. I offered to take away right now the burden of his handling our "eighty," but he insisted on continuing to serve as caretaker—part of his fatherly role. He passed me a packet of records pertaining to that land for me to look over. His daughter Lois told me later, yes, as long as possible he liked to feel needed; and being our land agent did just that.

Another thing: he'd never progressed as far as he'd hoped in sorting family memorabilia, which was to be mailed to each of us. I found my stack—a few letters from my year in Iran; copies of *The Mill*, the high school newspaper, of which I was editor; photographs of classmates and relatives; plus a lot of other stuff I hardly recognized but decided to haul away with me in order to show him my appreciation. In another section of the room his sisters' costume jewelry lay in old Christmas card boxes—interesting baubles from the twenties, which I knew my wife would like. "Take what you want," he said. "Only I'm keeping the gold watches. Each of us Pa gave a gold watch. I'm putting them in a case for display."

Luckily I made the visit when I did, for a few weeks after I returned to New York, Jack became worse and Lois placed him in a nursing home near the hospital in Le Mars, eleven miles away. I phoned, but he was never at ease talking long distance and now trying to speak in a corridor with others nearby made it even more of an ordeal. I mailed food parcels for Christmas and kept checking with Lois as to how he was faring. She mentioned his roommate, a cousin by marriage who had farmed a few miles away. One of the nurses on the staff had been a high school classmate of mine. All the nurturing that small-town lifetime acquaintances can give were in place and providing comfort.

Neighbor Nilles drove Jack back to the farm for a couple of visits, so that he could sit in the house and have a sense of still belonging there—see that everything was just as it had always been.

THOUGH ON SOCIAL SECURITY AND PARTIALLY RETIRED,
JACK CONTINUES TO FARM SOME OF THE LAND; 1960s.

His trappings of personality filled the place, mingling with those of
his parents and siblings and us children. Very understanding of that
neighbor to realize Jack would need a meditative period in this
setting. "I took longer at chores than I would have had to," Nilles
told me later. "To give him a little extra time in the house."

Sitting at the kitchen table with pencil and notepad, Jack wrote
down obituary facts about himself and funeral instructions to be
carried out "when the time comes." The coffin was to be oak, "unless
it's too expensive"; the hymn, "Abide with Me," which had been sung
at his wife Lizzie's funeral and probably at his two sons' services as
well. The sermon text would be from Isaiah: "Surely He hath borne
our griefs and carried our sorrows." He asked that the funeral be
conducted with the full military honors befitting a veteran of World
War I. The flowers he preferred—red roses—were to be distributed
afterwards to the Happy Fiesta Nursing Home in Remsen. The
headstone had long been in place in our family cemetery plot. Only
the concluding date needed to be chiseled in.

In February, a phone call from Nilles: "I don't know how much longer it's going to be for Jack. If you're planning on seeing him one more time, it better be soon."

I had a business trip to Detroit coming up and so booked a side excursion to Sioux City for a few days. At the airport there I picked up a rental car and drove the forty miles home, snow lying thick on the fields; but the roads were clear, no bad weather in the offing. As I swung into the farmyard, I felt the house looked higher and more worn out, abandoned of everything that had made it seem alive.

So now it's down to me, I thought, entering the kitchen, walking through the rooms. I have come to the very end of all this. I climbed the stairs to my old bedroom and brushed dead flies off the sheets and pillowslip; these very linens I had used on my previous visit. All night, though it was very quiet, I didn't sleep much.

Next morning in the nursing home I found Uncle Jack in a wheelchair in his room. "I never thought I'd end up in a place like this." He seemed humbled by his state, dishonored.

"Oh, it's not so bad, is it? If you need it."

"I need it all right. Tend a fella like a baby. Sometimes I feel like one. Can't do anything for myself no more."

I learned from my nurse friend that at first Jack had fought the institutional routines and refused to belong to this world of the nursing home. But finally he had "adjusted" and began to participate in afternoon entertainments and to attend the nondenominational church services on Sundays. I wondered how much the two cousins, now roommates, had to say to one another; maybe everything had been gone over years ago, living as they had three miles from each other for most of this century. A stranger as his roommate might have been better; Jack's old stories would have found a new and interested audience.

"Thing is, you've got to keep going. In your mind." He had set himself a particular goal: to live until his youngest grandson, Scott, graduated from high school in late May. Why he had become so fixed on that event, no one knew, though Lois mentioned he'd always felt especially close to Scott. "He wouldn't be well enough to attend commencement anyhow, I suppose," she said.

I remembered the teasing fun Jack always seemed to have with Scott. Once, after visiting me in New York, Jack's plane from Chicago's O'Hare airport to Sioux City was rescheduled to depart much later than expected. The family, waiting to meet him, took note of the posted delay and went off to shop for a couple of hours. However, they changed Jack's booking, routing him by way of Omaha with a plane transfer to Sioux City, and so he arrived with no one to greet him. When the family finally showed up, Scott rushed forward. "Grandpa! What are you doing here?" and Jack replied, grinning: "I beat the plane."

In the nursing home next day we made our falsely hearty goodbyes; then I returned to New York. A month later, Lois told me on the phone that Jack, now in the hospital, had awakened from a drug-induced sleep to ask, "He's graduated, hasn't he?"

I realized the end was surely near. Jack died May 2, and the town of Remsen's flag was lowered to half-mast. Long distance calls to relatives were made, and I flew home.

Obituaries appeared in both the *Sioux City Journal* and the county newspaper on the day before the funeral, giving ample local notice. Since this was spring-planting time, we thought many farmers would pay their respects at the wake in the funeral home the evening before rather than give up a precious morning of field work. The open coffin was set in an alcove heavy with the odor of roses; piped-in organ music played softly.

An old man's wake can be celebratory. People began arriving in late afternoon, wrote their names in the ledger—some leaving money in memorial envelopes—and I, along with other close family members, stood in the receiving line for the ritual handshake and "You have my sympathy." I felt strange being the recipient of this message, for I had been away so long and in some ways *I* should be offering sympathy to them, who had known Jack on a steady basis.

As they enter the funeral home I try to place them, recognizing some from my previous visits and hoping their names will come back. Here is Dora, the teacher who taught me to read phonetically in a one-room rural schoolhouse over fifty years ago; a neighbor boy kicked by a horse sometime in the thirties, still with his bleary eye and caved-in forehead; Jack's American Legion buddies; farmers' elevator associates; church friends. The talk almost drowns out the canned organ music. We are reaffirming family connections, work alliances, country ties—a rich slurry of time and events.

It rains the morning of the funeral. Farmers, now free to come in from the spring fields, fill Christ Lutheran church. Relatives gather in the basement to be assigned places in the procession to follow the coffin down the aisle: first Lois and Rex, then the two grandsons, me and my brother from California, another nephew and two nieces, the various cousins.

After the service the cortege of cars to the cemetery, headlights on, trails behind the hearse in this same order. We halt under the pines near the new grave, open fields all around. The wind-driven rain is cold; we huddle close under the canopy while the minister intones the final "ashes to ashes." The honor guard shoulders arms, fires three volleys, and the bugler blows taps. Exactly the ending he wanted.

Then back to the church, where the Ladies Aid hospitality committee has prepared lunch for 130 relatives and neighbors, many having traveled great distances. Time for visiting. Couldn't we get up a family reunion the way we used to; take over an entire state park? Remember those Fourth of July and New Year's Eve madcap parties—weren't they fun? Someone displays a chart tracing grandmother's people to the seventeenth century in Westphalia, Germany. Pieces begin to fit together in new ways. No, I didn't know that Aunt Elizabeth had paid the college tuition of her cousin's granddaughter, but now I understand why the little red-haired girl running around here is named Elizabeth. In the midst of talk I savor a rhubarb-custard pie, tart and creamy—haven't tasted one in years.

When the church basement finally empties, some of us pay calls in town on relatives too infirm to have been part of this day. My mother's stepsister, Mabel, ninety-two, tells me: "I felt closer to your mother than to my own sisters. We were exactly the same age—and both teachers."

My brother has to leave. I end up at Lois and Rex's farm for dinner, and we spend a long time in the vegetable and flower garden as evening approaches across the plains.

I have a last night in the old farmhouse, Uncle Jack's presence filling the rooms, even the familiar smell of him, everywhere. He had become as much a part of the farm as the three oak trees his sister Anna (later called Anne) planted when Grandfather broke the prairie sod. He was a rural populist, patriotic; he trusted society, served the community, and took care of his large family. There *were* moments when he complained about his straits, wished he had escaped this envelope of time and circumstances; but mostly he joined forces with his destiny and became proud of his long hold on the past as he

LIZZIE AND JACK, C. 1950.

carried it into the present.

I know all the reasons why I left this primal enclosure. I am free of family entanglements not of my choosing. Loners that most of us seem to be these days, with nuclear families or extended families of friends, we speak of "community" as something easy to latch onto or even make up. But a day like today made me realize that a community is either real or not there at all—just something we sometimes speak of as if it were.

Many of us Midwesterners fled relatives and hometowns because life couldn't be accepted in a predecided manner but had to be discovered, each on his or her own. However, a time such as this may come when one is suddenly thrown back to origins, with witnesses all around saying: We know who *you* are, and you know who *we* are; let us examine, accept, and even embrace this moment before it too passes.

Lois inherited the farmhouse and the 160-acre homestead, but it was too late in her life to start farming there with Rex. Used to a smaller house, she did not fancy the housekeeping necessary in this place. Furthermore, she and Rex (she fifty-three, he fifty-seven) were thinking of taking things a little easier before long. She was enrolled in courses leading to a master-gardener citation, and she spoke of returning to her brushes and paints—perhaps even setting up a studio. Farm scenes painted on old saws were a popular gift item these days; she planned to do a few in acrylics by way of experiment.

Lois and Rex's choice of semiretirement residence was his mother's home in the country—a sturdily constructed 1929 bungalow—a few miles from where they had been living. (Rex's mother had died a few months before Jack.) By adding a room to make a proper kitchen, the house would do just fine.

Our old home now needed to be made suitable for a renter to move in as soon as possible, for security reasons. There were lots of empty farmhouses in this part of the country and finding someone might be difficult. The tenant would not be farming the surrounding land, for Nilles had contracts on all of it. The house clean-out could take at least a week, Lois thought. But during the summer she and her husband simply did not have the time, given the demands of the farm.

In September the Nilleses came up with a young couple they thought Lois would approve of. These days one had to be so careful, Lois told me on the phone. Sometimes young couples into drugs liked to be off by themselves in the country, where nobody could check on what they were up to. They often made a terrible wreck of a house before anyone caught onto them. But the Nilleses felt sure this young pair would not be like that.

When could the house be emptied? Lois and Rex immediately set about disposing of most of the furnishings. They were either saved for the family or carried off by a secondhand dealer who arrived with a truck. Not much cash for the furniture; these were depression days in farm country. Our utilitarian pieces weren't old enough to be considered antiques or in good enough shape to interest substantial buyers. "I hope you don't mind what we did," Lois said to me on the phone, "but there wasn't a choice really, since we have to turn over the place empty."

I regretted the loss of none of it. Items like most of those could be picked up at sales almost any time, should nostalgia overcome me. Furthermore, there was still the entire attic to be gone over, chock-full of family trash and saved items. I promised to fly out and help when she was ready.

The renters the Nilleses had lined up understood that we would be taking care of the attic soon, in early fall. But as the beginning of October neared, their projected moving-in date, they decided not to take the place after all, for when the rooms were broom-clean, the

LOIS, NOW AN ART TEACHER,
SHORTLY BEFORE HER MARRIAGE,
LATE 1950s.

house seemed absolutely enormous. On the first floor, twelve-foot high stamped-tin ceilings; then a steep staircase to the big rooms on the second floor. How could they afford to furnish a house this size? And the expense of heating it! But mostly, the housewife felt the place was "spooky"; she knew she couldn't live in it.

Emptying the attic would be much easier, I felt, not having a family already installed. We could sort out things in downstairs rooms and toss boxes out of attic windows. We might make a mess, and it wouldn't matter.

In November, corn picking over, Lois decided now was the time to confront the attic; could I fly out? "Dress up warm," she said on the phone, as if New York living had made me forget Iowa weather. "There's no heat in the house."

The day after I arrived on a late night-flight, we drove up from Lois and Rex's farm and set to work. Lorne Nilles had been keeping his dairy cows in the grove to munch on brush and keep down the orchard grass as well as clip the lawns. The familiar tangled thickets out there, once beloved by birds, were gone. The ravages of that tornado three years before were painfully apparent from the many half-fallen trees. I could look right through the grove to the wide western horizon. The house was now plainly visible from the road, standing high and Victorian—a little Charles Addams-like spooky, the unpainted tin roof shaped in steep gables.

We unlocked the front entrance and walked slowly through the echoing, empty rooms, which had lost much of their Harnack family resonance. Paint hung in curls from the ceilings. The burled pine woodwork, never painted out of respect for Grandfather, was now fully exposed and looked badly in need of refinishing. Our old home had become merely a house. The suddenness of the transformation surprised me, and I felt myself to be a relic from another life.

Oh-oh; something wrong at the attic door. The lock turned okay, but the steps leading up were strewn with dusty hats, children's books, and checkerboard pieces. Thieves had gotten here ahead of us, jimmied open the attic door. Lois noticed that her mother's cedar chest was gone. I realized that Mother's trunk wasn't where it always stood at the head of the stairs; my father's silver shaving stand was missing, too.

After we'd gotten over our first shock, Lois said: "Hard to know what's stolen when we don't know what all was here in the first place."

We were on a mission to rid the building of contents—take it away, sell, or keep it—not too different from what the marauders had done; but still, the violation was unsettling. The house had never before been burglarized. Lois and Rex had some ideas who might have done it, though they didn't elaborate.

What action could be taken? We couldn't provide the police with a list of items taken; and any smart thieves would dispose of the stolen goods at some distance.

So on with the task at hand. The attic was in the shape of a giant T. We moved slowly up and down the three narrow aisles, trying to figure out how to begin, how to organize this dismemberment. Fortunately, the foot-pump parlor organ was already in the local Heritage Center museum, as well as Grandfather's Montgomery Ward mahogany love seat and green plush chair. Grandmother's spinning wheel, a walnut desk and bookcase made by Grandfather, a set of handpainted china, and a Victorian fainting couch in crimson velvet had been disposed of to friends and family.

The only way to view this project was to think of it as the culmination of those years when as children we wanted to play in the attic but were so carefully monitored that we never had a chance to get into much mischief up here. We never really explored all the booty the attic might contain.

The bearing beam was about ten feet high at the peak, with the rafters sloping all the way down to the floor at the outer edges; a great deal could be stored in this place without difficulty. Down below, the burled pine door to the attic looked as handsome as any in the building, as if Grandfather had surmised how important the top of the house would become in our lives.

Behind the door, the stairs began immediately, rising straight up. Since the steps could be used as a sort of receding series of shelves, we kept the supply of toilet paper handy there. The wood remained in its raw, unfinished state, but for some reason the plastered and painted stairwell had been decorated with a stenciled border of pine cones and boughs found nowhere else in the house. In my young days this intrigued me. A talisman of some sort; a trail marker? Inside the attic door a string dangled, attached to a naked light bulb high in the center of the roof—the only illumination in the entire loft, except for the small, square-paned windows at each gable.

We began: gauzy dust masks over our noses giving us a disguise for meeting whatever ghosts might rise up in indignation. College textbooks, pennants—discard; aluminum cream-separator parts—saleable; a small globe I'd won in a high school current events contest—toss out (I'd been all over this world by now); boxes of Parker games from the thirties and forties—keep, presents for the grandchildren; Lois's brother Donald's Air Force uniform and the flag that had draped his coffin—she saved it, of course; Father's cracked sheepskin coat—out; a hank of reddish braided hair snipped off during the flapper craze—we try not to identify whose, so that it can be thrown away; a toy wooden elephant and jointed pig, highly saleable; German language Sunday School books, pamphlets describing pantomimes, anagram games—(we're now in the nineteenth century) save. Members of the family become vivid as these artifacts call them back, but to what purpose? Only to be laid to rest forever, out the window or down the stairs and away from the house.

On a farm there is no Goodwill pickup or garbage service. When someone died, clothes and personal items, often in dressers containing them, were simply hauled up to the attic to await an emotionally calmer time—which never came. We also stashed belongings in the attic when we moved on to college or jobs in distant cities. On visits home I would paw through boxes of my effects, only to walk away without cleaning up the past. These siftings of family life felt cozy emotionally; I knew where I came from and what still remained here. Thirteen children in two generations had grown up in this house, and each of them left something behind.

Exhausted at day's end, Lois, Rex, and I returned to their home and spent the evening sorting through photographs, trying to identify them. But for whom? Her sons weren't interested any more than I'd been in ancestors unknown. The farmhouse no longer served our purposes, and neither did these photo images. Yet, we knew that the secrets of all our lives lay in that attic—which was why, I realized, nobody had wanted to touch any of it.

THE GLORIOUS FOURTH

Did you ever think you and me would be doing this?" Lois asked, on our second day. "That finally it would be—just you and me?"

"Yeah, because we were the youngest." When we were little, we were both put into the same bathtub on Saturday nights to save water during the drought years of the 1930s.

She picked up an old newspaper from a nearby stack.

"Oh, don't throw that one out," I said. "Look at the headline."

FOURTH OF JULY FIRE

"Remember when half the town of Remsen burned down?"

"Do I ever."

During the worst Depression years of the early thirties, civil disobedience—and occasional riots—were frequent throughout Iowa because so many were losing their farms. The idea of nationhood seemed to have become so feeble for most people that to have a holiday like the Fourth of July for patriotic reassertion (Armistice Day was another) gave us children the sense of being connected to something larger: to the country as a whole.

Weeks before the holiday, Uncle Jack paid serious attention to his fireworks mail order, almost as if it were his birthday we would be celebrating along with that of the United States. He took his allegiance to the flag very seriously, and on holidays one of us would be delegated to hang a large flag from hooks between the pillars of the front porch, just in case anybody drove into the yard who might see it. The point was, *we* were aware of it on display there. And on Monday nights in spring, fall, and winter, Uncle Jack would undertake a patriotic rite by donning his blue Legionnaire's cap with gold piping and attend meetings in the American Legion Hall. However, too many of the Rainbow Division veterans merely sat around "grousing and drinking beer" in the smoke-heavy room, forgetting obligations to "do something for your country."

Our stock of fireworks, ammunition to win this day all over again for Independence, arrived in late June: garish packages and crates with large-lettered scary warnings that hung from our mailbox flag or projected from the open box. This shipment could never be mistaken for an ordinary order from Sears, Roebuck. We would cluster around Jack as he cut the wire bindings and ripped open the parcels, checking to make sure the entire order was intact. The crinkly, crimson tissue paper inside was like the vestments of Chinese gunpowder masters, as mysterious as the kimono-colored paper flowers that burst open in glasses of water.

"Yep, everything's here," he'd say, counting the tubular skyrockets nestled together like sticks of dynamite; the packets of firecrackers in graded sizes; and the glossy torpedoes, smooth as golf balls. "We're in good shape."

"You sure spent plenty for 'em," Lizzie or Mother might remark, frowning. "Don't leave those fireworks in the house! Take 'em out to the summer kitchen or the cob shed." Worried lest one of us lose an eye or blow off a finger. They enjoyed the family gathering on the Fourth and making a feast—everything except these sinister explosives, which to us seemed the chief feature.

The morning of the holiday, the youngest among us seven received harmless ladyfingers from Jack's depot, plus a short stick of punk, but we couldn't even scare the cats with the tiny smack they made. For the older boys, the ordnance supplies included fat firecrackers called "number ones," to be set off in tin cans ("depth charges"), and torpedoes, that exploded when thrown on the sidewalk.

We played war all day, whirling our sparklers across the lawn, dancing away from the glittering sparks that never seemed to hurt when they fell on bare toes. Turretlike pipes protruded from the edges of the cistern lid, perfect for inserting medium-sized firecrackers and firing away as if defending a fortress. The yard soon smelled of fire and brimstone, the dog cowered under the kitchen porch, and we were all having one hell of a good time.

The daytime noise extravaganza would be followed by a visual night show of "the rocket's red glare." But since every army travels on its stomach, we tucked into the tray supper on the screened-in porch and savored the custard ice cream made with ice which had been cut from the horsetank half a year ago. Today the blackened cakes shaped like rocks from the earth and crusted with decomposed sawdust had been dug out of the icehouse, dripping winter weather. We chipped the block, packed slivers around the cylinder, salted the slush, and the child most diligent at the crank handle always got to lick the dasher in the end.

Most other holidays had something wrong with them: Christmas meant toys of course, but also long passages to memorize in the church pageant and the chance of making a fool of oneself before the whole congregation. Thanksgiving invariably started with morning church services and doleful warnings from the pulpit about being too smug in the feasting, since others in the country were starving. Easter lost its charm when we discovered the bunny didn't exist—at nearly the same time confirmation proceedings began and a testing before the minister, which was as trying as school examinations. On Memorial Day we would mow grass on cemetery graves and mourn the dear departed ones. Labor Day was the awful start of school. It seemed that only New Year's Eve and the Fourth of July were devoted purely to fun; with joy untempered, our reach could exceed our grasp.

A chief participant in these two holiday celebrations was Mother and Lizzie's only full brother, Uncle Frank, who had converted to Catholicism upon his marriage to blue-eyed Irish Bess. Since the Fourth and New Year's Eve were the only major holidays untainted by religion, these were suitable secular occasions for family get-togethers. Catholics, by nature of their special bonds to Rome, were thought to live quite different lives from ours. They enjoyed more pleasures, for one thing, living easily among boozers and gamblers in card-playing circles, freely committing sins. Merely "fell on their knees" Sunday after Sunday in a suspicious posture of repentance. No effort seemed spent at individual soul-searching and self-examination of deeds, which Martin Luther had suggested *we* do. The only way our family could hold together as relatives should was to ignore the entire religious business. And we did, with Uncle Frank and his family.

We seldom had his company except on these holidays. He exuded an irrepressible gaiety, brought on by the birth of the new year or the birth of our country. "Uncle Frank's full of the dickens," everyone said. He could mimic a neighbor's self-pitying tone or a fool's bloated opinions in a voice like Charlie McCarthy's—throat-swallowed and gargly.

Just as his Catholicism showed us there were other ways of subscribing to God's intentions, so his red hair illustrated the wild gene in our blood which might have unexpected consequences: we might produce redhaired babies some day. He had lost most of that carrot hair by the time I knew him, but his dome added still another facet to the possible surprises in store for us males, since no other close relatives were bald.

We would squeal with joy when Uncle Frank smacked his lips and rolled his eyes, Buster Keaton fashion, or yelped, pulling out an unexpected winning card in the game of High-Low-Jack-and-the-Dame, which he taught us to play during the midnight vigil of a New Year's Eve. His humor lay in the risible grip he had upon the world, monitoring the funny doings of everyone—an irony of such proportion that he seemed to have hold of the cosmic laugh itself. But Frank's later years were bitter for no reason any of us could figure out, unless he felt he was paying for his laughter—that the last one would be on *him*.

Frank, Bess, and their three children would arrive around six P.M. on the Fourth of July, after they had finished farm chores—and we had done ours. Bright-colored boxes were hauled from Uncle Frank's car trunk. We always pooled our supplies in order to have a display so spectacular that neighbors for miles around would say how they enjoyed watching the skyrockets zoom into the night high above our thick grove.

Soon after the ice cream was exhausted, the cake and other comestibles eaten, the men and older boys eagerly began to assemble the artillery. Pieces of an old downspout made fine ramps for launching the two-foot rockets. Roman candles were placed on high wire stems and planted in the lawn like croquet wickets.

Suspense mounted as the dusk deepened; darkness was necessary for the full effect. The women remained on the screened-in porch, well out of danger should a corkscrew, stray rocket come sizzling that way. *Oh! Ahh!* from the watchers as each successful rocket soared into the empyrean, higher than our tallest cottonwood,

UNCLE FRANK, FUN-LOVING HOST
OF OUR FOURTH OF JULY AND
NEW YEAR'S EVE PARTIES.

exploding up there into a fountain of multicolored stars. There were always a few duds Uncle Jack said he would send back to the firecracker company but of course never did. And no matter how long the glorious racket and spangled show went on, we could never accept the end, that it was over, that somewhere in the tissue paper of the crates we couldn't find one more.

In the drought years, fireworks might set ablaze the brown lawns or parched groves; a measly ladyfinger could start a dreaded prairie fire, tales of which we'd heard from older relatives. These days the stunted oats fields and fired cornstalks could become the tinder that the tall prairie grass had been in nineteenth-century conflagrations.

One Independence Day, perhaps 1935, it was 105° at noon as we slurped cool pink watermelon in the shade-drawn kitchen of the farmhouse. The melon had been chilled in the cistern in a gunnysack suspended by a rope. An undercurrent of fire-worry among the adults put a damper on our fun. When we gathered in the evening at Uncle Frank's farm six miles away, the question was still unresolved as to whether or not we should go ahead with the rocket display because of the fire hazard. We prayed that the rain forecaster's promise would come true in time for us to have a safe fireworks orgy.

Thunderheads began to darken the sunset sky soon after our arrival. We had a splendid view of the foaming blue-black clouds, since Uncle Frank's grove was spindly. "Tornado! Tornado!" someone yelled—the most terrifying word in our vocabulary.

"Where? Where?" the women called from the house. "Coming our way?"

"Looks like it," said Uncle Jack. "Everybody better get down cellar."

I saw the twister weave and dance across the cornfields to the southwest, a dark funnel wobbling toward us. Immediately our whole clan scrambled for the basement, which I soon discovered was much smaller than ours at home. The safest place was along the western wall, for if the house were lifted up and carried away, the suction would be least in the bunker facing the direction of attack. No sooner were we secure and ready for the onslaught than I felt impatient to have it over. How long would it take for the storm to get here? What should we do with ourselves in the meantime, squashed together against the damp cement wall? Because there were two families, the multitude assembled in close quarters gave an eerie seriousness to the event, such as the representatives of all the species of life crowded into the Ark must have felt.

Uncle Frank peered down upon us from the trapdoor overhead, like the Joker from the playing deck in Shoot the Moon. He laughed and pointed—we were the funniest-looking bunch he'd ever seen—almost as if he'd planned the tornado in order to make us all look ridiculous, crouching in that burrow.

"Close the door, Frank, and come down here!" one of his sisters called.

During the suspenseful quiet just before the storm hit, Uncle Frank secretly threw an enormous firecracker into a basement window. When the thing exploded—a tremendous bang so near it seemed the crack of doom—we shrieked in terror. His laughter fell upon us almost at the same moment an avalanche of rain struck the house. The tornado had missed us; spared once more. In addition, the ground was now so thoroughly drenched that there would be no need to hold back our celebration, once the lightning ceased giving competition to our skyrockets and the thunder stopped trying to outdo our biggest firecrackers.

In 1936 the drought was so severe that our lawns were the color of the Baltimore oriole's nest swinging in the birch tree. On the Fourth of July the corn was only an adolescent's knee high, and the oats and barley acres were stunted from lack of moisture. Midmorning of the holiday, a little girl in Remsen, playing with her sparkler, set fire to a box of rags in the rear of her father's restaurant. They tried to put it out themselves after sounding the alarm, but soon the wooden cafe was entirely in flames. Downwind, the whole town began to go up in flames. Gasoline tanks along the railroad tracks exploded like oversize Roman candles, sending huge black columns of smoke into the air; the grain elevators became great torches.

We hopped into our 1934 Ford and raced to the scene, two and a half miles away, leaving our firecracker child's play for this, the real thing. Grandma lived on the edge of town and was probably safe, but we hoped to help save Aunt Bertha's millinery shop on the main street.

Nothing the fire engines could do, even those hailing from neighboring cities, dampened the relentless course of that Fourth of July fire. The intensity of the flames, added to the heat of the day, buckled sidewalks, caved in walls, and gave us all a foretaste of hell. The saloons in the north end of town were swept out of existence, as if the Lord's hand had fallen upon them at last. All of the downtown business section appeared headed for damnation.

We hauled away as much of Aunt Bertha's drygoods stock as we could salvage: boxes of elaborate hats; feathers standing straight on end as if excited from an old bird-fear of fire; dummies the size of people, with clothes partially clinging to them; metal racks holding swishy dresses, the fabric covering our nostrils and filtering the smoke. From the oak-and-glass display cases we dumped costume jewelry, hairpin cards, fancywork yarns, buttons, and other female accoutrements into wicker laundry hampers and storeroom cardboard cartons. Finally Jack said it was getting too dangerous to go back inside for more, and so with our last carload we drove off. The roof was ablaze, and although Bertha's shop was on the ground floor, it would be only a matter of minutes before the ceiling beams collapsed. All the rest of her stock was lost and she didn't have insurance. But the following year she relocated in smaller quarters across the street, for she still had a wide following of women customers, eager to stop in and hear the latest. Her biggest resource could never be destroyed by fire.

For weeks afterward the grain elevators smoldered and stank, the biggest punk imaginable. Our town looked as if it hadn't survived the rocket's red glare, the bombs bursting in air. And all from a little kid's sparkler! Later in school we nicknamed her "Sparkle Plenty" after the girl in "Dick Tracy." By then the state legislature in Des Moines had passed a bill banning private use of fireworks. None was to be sold to Iowa residents from out-of-state sources, either, under penalty of law. From now on the Fourth would be observed sanely, with community fireworks under safe, controlled conditions.

We talked of ways we might have another real Fourth: maybe we should drive to South Dakota, buy contraband fireworks on the sly, and smuggle them home, across the Big Sioux River. Like all country men, we bridled at government interference in our freedom to do as we pleased—even burn ourselves up. However, the great town bonfire subtly consumed our future interest in the whole matter of firecrackers, aided by Mother and Lizzie's "See, we told you so!" They were greatly relieved to have an end to the dangerous racket.

On succeeding Independence Days, we would pile into our car and drive like other tame and gelded good citizens to the public fireworks in the park of Le Mars, the county seat, though I don't think Uncle Frank and his family bothered to go. We hoped the show put on by the Le Mars Chamber of Commerce might include unusual, expensive rockets—perhaps the flag in red, white, and blue, with shooting stars. However, the affair seemed labored, with long pauses between rockets and too many sputtering, lifeless Roman candles.

Then, hardly before we knew how it happened, firecrackers were transformed into the real thing. America found itself on the ramparts once more, and the four males in our family took up arms for our country in World War II. Soon the biting odor of gunpowder came to signify death for somebody; the rockets whining through the air meant bombs blowing up cities.

Neither we nor the nation ever got over it—back into a pastoral Fourth-of-July birthday mood as innocent of war as Chinese noisemakers ushering in their New Year. Not with the Korean conflict following so closely after the nuclear explosions over Hiroshima and Nagasaki and then the awful war in Vietnam. Asia, source of gunpowder centuries ago, seemed to be claiming back from us all the joyful simpleness we once had. Or perhaps with our literal, Western-minded absorption in the mechanics of explosives, we have forgotten metaphorical gunpowder.

Once upon a time we citizens felt impelled to demonstrate with Fourth-of-July hoopla that America had been strong enough to make a country for itself, and the smallest popping ladyfinger suggested the shots fired at Lexington and Concord. Now nobody in the world needed to be told.

MULBERRIES

Here was a Remsen *Bell-Enterprise,* carefully saved; was one of us in it? Extra copies of an issue containing a family obituary were often laid away in their brown wrappers by way of reverent memorial. I can seldom resist poring over an old newspaper, but it would be a time-consuming diversion leading me away from the task at hand.

The editor of the *Bell* occasionally revealed a coarse, frontier-style humor. He planted one-liners between news stories such as: "In the spring the busy housewife sits among her cabbages and peas."

He relished a court case involving a woman who owned a pure-bred boar for stud purposes. The woman was sued for damages by a neighbor whose sow was impregnated after the boar crashed through a fence. In the trial the woman testified that her fence was sound; the neighbor should not have had his sow, who was in heat, running around loose if he expected to control her breeding. "How do you know the sow was in heat?" asked the judge. The woman replied: "When a sow's rear end is red as the sun going down, *anything* will jump the fence." She won the case.

Now I tilted the yellowing front page of a *Bell* to catch the cobwebby light through the attic window. "What have you found?" Lois asked.

"Ah . . . here it is." I began to read aloud:

William Milfs, 54, Takes Own Life

William Milfs, 54, lifelong Remsen resident, was found dead in the basement of his mother's home about 8 a.m. Monday by Kenneth

Portz, a mechanic at the Ross Motor
Co.
        Sheriff   Frank   Scholer   and
County   Coroner   S.   H.   Lucken
investigated   and   termed   the   death
suicide   by   strangulation.   Mr.   Milfs
hanged   himself   with   a   plastic
clothesline   from   a   basement   pipe.
. . .   When   he   did   not   show   up   for
work   Monday   morning,   Mr.   Portz
went   to   the   Milfs   home,   noticed   a
light   burning   in   the   basement   and
discovered the body.
        Unmarried,   Milfs   had   made   his
home with his mother . . .

I stopped. "But I seem to remember a wife and children."

"You're thinking of the brother, Milf Milfs. *He* was the one used
to drive out to see Dad."

Scanning the list of survivors, I note four brothers, among them
Milf, living in California. "Milf Milfs; so he really *did* have a name
like that!" A comic-strip character's moniker—like Moon Mullins.

"Wasn't Milf Milfs a friend of Jack's?" I said, remembering a
Milfs girl exactly Lloyd's age—and that Lizzie had been in the
hospital giving birth to him when Mrs. Milfs was lying in. We often
heard how winter came exceptionally early in 1924, the roads shut by
a blizzard just when Lizzie needed to be off to the hospital in Le
Mars. With a team pulling a sled, she and Jack made it to the
Remsen depot, where they caught a train. After Lloyd's birth,
November 25, it was bitterly cold; Jack and Lizzie worried about the
infant's safety on the sled ride home. They asked the doctor's advice
on how they should manage it, for wouldn't the baby suffocate if
covered up completely? Yet if Lloyd weren't wrapped securely, he
wouldn't survive the extreme cold.

"Oh, the baby won't smother," the doctor said, "if you arrange
the blanket so there's a hole right above the nose. Then put your
finger down through the opening and touch his nose. That'll keep out
the cold but give him enough space to breathe."

The whole way home, baby Lloyd had a finger touching his
nose—connected to his mother no longer with an umbilical cord but
something just as good.

"Didn't Milf Milfs and his family used to pick our mulberries?"

I asked.

"Mulberries!" Lois said. "Yes, *we* never bothered with them."

Taste and smells have the longest, surest hold on memory, and I could never forget the flat, insipid taste of the despised berry. It brought back a midsummer night of long ago—perhaps a composite of summer evenings on the farm in the thirties, when nestled together as a family on the big screened-in porch, we felt protected from whatever threatened in the outside world.

The rhythmic creak of the porch swing, suspended by two strong chains from the ceiling, maintained a beat through a lull in the talk, almost like a heart. Kept on going and going as if it would never stop.

"Look—the moon!" a child said, perhaps Lois or me. The deep orange glow behind the machine shed began to brighten. Everyone watched in silence as the light increased, waiting for the orb to appear. Behind panels of screen that stood firmly in place between the white pillars to keep mosquitoes out, we attended to the moon's rising as if it needed our concentration in order to succeed in climbing the night sky.

Bertha and Elizabeth sat on the orange-and-green striped canvas swing, with a passel of nephews and nieces sprawled around them—on laps, next to thighs and hips; a closeness of family flesh, and these two spinsters craved it. Being Jack's older sisters, they made providential use of the farm whenever they felt like it—especially in summers when Elizabeth was home on vacation from teaching typing and shorthand in a Detroit high school.

The field garden had been planted in early May with the aunts' additional needs in mind. No patch of soil in the ordinary vegetable garden plots near the house would be big enough for all of us. Each year a small piece of a cornfield was set aside for the major vegetable garden.

Several times a week after supper, Elizabeth and Bertha would take advantage of the long evening light and drive out, wearing funny old dresses and smocks—"real garden-working clothes." They weeded a little, as if none of us children assigned the task had done it well enough, and harvested whatever crop might be ready. One could sense their partial ownership of the farm during these visits, for they reverted to being "the girls" again. Later on the porch, with refreshments in the offing (Lizzie an unfailing hostess), memories of

LLOYD AND LOIS WITH THEIR AUNT ELIZABETH, 1935.

"Pa" and "Ma" and the antics of "the boys" would spill out—tales frequently retold since we children begged for them, though we knew every inflection, having heard all of this many times before. We were wrapping ourselves in layers of safety, for family tales can shelter the young. What happened is over; yet the retelling keeps it alive, and we live through our legends.

On this particular night Lizzie had not yet served "the drink," and someone had finished a particularly funny story. "Ha! That was a good one," Bertha said, going over the yarn in her head, a chuckle still rattling around in her throat. Bertha's aftershocks from a story often lasted for a time as she wrung out the last bit of merriment—and seemed to be encouraging someone to begin another.

Her brother Jack lay sprawled like a mountainous island on the bare porch floor, his head supported by a lumpy pillow from the swing. My mother, Carrie, in the wicker rocker, said little all evening, except to reiterate as someone always did that it was a blessing to have a porch on a hot night, because of the breeze blowing up off the lawn. In these Depression years her financial means, derived from Father's insurance policy, became the family cash resource, which nicely coincided with a debt-free farm, where we were almost self-sufficient in food. Carrie's manner within the family was a curious blend of quiet strength and self-effacement.

In the swing the boys with the longest legs reached down and pushed with bare toes, providing the locomotion. The rest of us enjoyed the lolling ride, looking out at the stars over the cottonwood trees, watching the moon rise, feeling the breeze from the southwest, where the chill began in the hollows.

There was a long pause, marked not so much by the fact that no one had anything further to say as that our thoughts seemed held in common and no words needed to be spoken. Our minds, bodies, and spirits were too interconnected in this dark, warm moment for us to break things apart by casual talk or an attempt to re-establish individual identities.

Then a car swung into the roadgate, headlights flashing along the ground and up under the trees. Laddie barked furiously and ran forward to menace the intruders, though he remained behind the front-yard picket fence. Jack stood up at once and scrutinized the vehicle, which was dimly visible because of the moon and the glare of headlights. "By golly, I think that's Milfs."

"Who? Who?" Voices in the dark.

"Milf Milfs; it's his car, all right." Without stopping to slip into shoes, Jack lumbered barefoot out to the gate at the end of the sidewalk. Being gregarious, Jack was eager to welcome company of almost any sort; and now he was particularly pleased to have a visit from his machine-shop buddy, who had never been here before. Milf with his mechanical skills would be a refreshing change after the solitary routine of a day cutting oats—only interesting when something went wrong with the binder or tractor.

"Hope he'll invite the Mrs. in," Lizzie said, rising from her chair. She had seen little of the woman since their hospital stay, partly because the Milfs family belonged to a different church.

Bertha and Elizabeth said nothing, but one could sense their displeasure. The creaking stopped because the boys pushing the swing were wondering what to do now that unexpected company had arrived. We were all astir in our snug nest and ready to scramble;

country mice at heart. Sometimes when strangers popped in we would run out the back door and into the grove to hide behind trees or in the chokecherry clumps.

"Look, they're getting out," someone said. Occasionally visitors remained seated and talked through the rolled-down windows, if it was just a short call.

"Dear, dear . . . what could they want?" Elizabeth hated this interruption.

"Hey, Mom!" Jack called from the Milfses' car. "Get that sheet once, will you?"

"Sheet?" Lizzie shot back, in the familiar penetrating voice that could be heard above the wind. "What sheet you mean?"

"For shaking Juneberries."

"Oh . . . run get it, one of you kids. It's on the back porch, folded up."

The Juneberries had already been harvested, the spindly trunks shaken in our fists as wildly as we could in order to make the purple fruit fall. The birds had snatched a goodly share, but the prolific mulberry trees seemed to lure them away; unaccountably, the birds preferred mulberries to Juneberries. Every year Lizzie canned Juneberry-and-cherry sauce, a favorite dessert in winter, and also put up jars of tart Juneberry jelly.

"Wonder what in the world they could want with that sheet," Bertha muttered.

"At *this* hour of night, yet!" from Elizabeth.

In the moonlight we saw Mrs. Milfs, wearing a light-colored housedress, walk away from the car with her two children, Milf and Jack following.

"Where do you suppose they're going?" Lizzie had planned to serve lemonade soon, ice cubes tinkling in a big glass pitcher. Were there enough lemons to stretch the drink? The Frigidaire, with its trays of ice cubes, was such a luxury after years of making do with the wonky kerosene icebox on the back porch.

"Go out and play with the Milfs children, why don't you—Curtis, Kenny?" Mother said from her rocker, gently. Just a suggestion to help us in our social development, which was always a bit at peril in this farm isolation.

We didn't move from the swing.

"Whatever do you suppose?" Bertha began. "They seem near the cowbarn, na'h?"

"There go the older boys with more sheets. They'll find out," said Mother.

We waited in silence. The moon brightened the landscape as if promising to illuminate this unexpected theater. The creaking of the swing had totally stopped; the whole house seemed to be listening.

"What's that sound?" someone asked.

A swishing noise, followed by a pattering like rain on a tin roof.

"They're shaking the white mulberry tree," said Lizzie with a laugh of relief. She sank back in her chair.

"Why don't the rest of you kids run help them?" Mother suggested again, half-heartedly.

"Funny time to shake mulberries." Elizabeth's voice held an unmistakable note of superiority. Here our family was, in a proper rhythm, knowing what was what. When and how. Strengths evolved from knowing so much *for sure*. Other people didn't.

"How can they see?" Bertha grumbled, taking her cue from her sister.

"Jack told Milf," Lizzie said, "that they could come out if they wanted mulberries. That was weeks ago. Wonder if the birds left 'em any?"

"Even using flashlights," Elizabeth went on, "they'll get a lot of sticks, worms, and whatnot—all scooped together in their pots and pans."

"Why would anybody want mulberries?" Lois asked; or maybe I did.

"*We* don't eat 'em," one of us added.

"But some people do," said Mother.

Elizabeth carefully delivered a simple, declarative sentence: "I don't like mulberries."

"Neither do I! Neither do I!" A virtual chorus from the swing.

Bertha's laugh erupted—she couldn't control it. "Don't like 'em myself."

With that over, we worked our toes to the floor again and the squeak of the swing filled the air with a regular beat. At least once a night somebody would remark, "Ought to get out the oil can; listen to that squeak," but nobody ever did.

"I used to make mulberry jam," said Lizzie, who never allowed the aunts to take over completely. None of us reminded Lizzie that those jars were the last to be consumed during winter.

"Ma threw mulberries in pies," Bertha said suddenly, as if it had just occurred to her after so many years.

"But only a few," argued Elizabeth.

"Oh, quite a few."

"We *never* had mulberry pies."

"Why, Ma would mix 'em with cherries and Juneberries; you probably never noticed."

"If you squeeze lemon juice over mulberries for a little tartness," Lizzie went on, serenely above what seemed a sisterly spat, "they come out real good. In pies or sauce."

"Mulberry sauce!" Elizabeth said. "Tasteless stuff, *I* always thought." She laughed, enjoying her own nerve in speaking the truth to anybody at all times. Outspokenness was one of the qualities she was most proud of—and admired for by her sisters.

"But why do the birds love 'em so?" I asked. The mulberry grove would be full of robins, brown thrashers, grackles, and redheaded woodpeckers, all of them pulling on the glossy berries that looked so tempting but which had a green, stemlike taste. For weeks during mulberry season it was hazardous walking barefoot; the bird droppings everywhere were wine and white, like globs of mixed paint. But I was also thinking that with all the fruit in season right now—strawberries, cherries, red raspberries and black, and soon the dew berries and blackberries—it seemed strange that anyone would care enough to arrive fairly late at night and shake mulberry trees. Some folks, I figured, couldn't resist taking what's free, no matter what.

"If you cut up rhubarb to mix with mulberries, that works too." Lizzie spoke with authority in the cooking department.

"Maybe it seems pretty good because you can't taste the mulberries, only rhubarb," Elizabeth said. Bertha, appreciating the frankness, began her backup laugh again.

"If the Milfs family wants to bother, that's fine isn't it?" Mother asked.

"Oh sure, if they don't know no better." Bertha's lapse in grammar was meant to give a punch to her retort. She spoke out of the smugness of home ownership, for every summer these two sisters not only took a share of the field garden and the orchard produce but also eggs and anything else available, by right of their having once lived here.

"I wonder why you *shake* mulberries," I began musingly, but you *pick* cherries.

The family found such queries exasperating because I wasn't really expecting an answer. I tended to blurt out whatever popped into my head that seemed to call for a response, though if someone took me up on it, I would stare absently and not listen. Perhaps now the explanation to me would be calmly matter-of-fact: berries with fragile stems might be shaken loose but not fruit with firm stems. Yet I'd be yearning for something a bit more metaphysical, skewed off to the side of the mundane, perhaps shooting away into nothing. With the world all too full of the ordinary, I liked a leaping off point into the different and perhaps inexplicable, where strangeness and wonder hovered and life *really* was.

When the Milfs family finished with the white mulberry tree, they moved toward the mulberry grove, Jack leading the way and the older boys tagging along. I hungered to spy on them, sneak up behind trees and watch them at work in the moonlight.

Grandfather had planted the mulberry trees as a windbreak against southwest gales. Now the old, gnarly stand sheltered a fenced stockyard, about an acre.

Over the years the trees had grown so tall that no one could harvest their fruit easily. Yet very little brush grew beneath the mulberries, whose trunk bark was rubbed glossy from pigs and cattle scratching their hides. Birds, discouraged by the strong wind, tended to shun the trees; but if they did nest there, they built tightly and securely between crotches.

Under those wind-noisy mulberries, you were almost to the fields, where you could gaze across miles of distant farmlands. Along the fencerow in the thick grass, meadowlarks and dickcissels nested. The soil here had never been broken by a plow or planted in crops; it was part of the original prairie.

At last I was too curious to remain where I was, and once off the porch a sibling joined me, the dew in the grass cool on our bare feet. We knew this territory like Indians, and as we crept through the grove, sleepy birds roused themselves and chirped plaintively. A robin, fully awake, perhaps enlivened by the moonlight, said "Speak! Speak!" and flew clumsily to a cottonwood bough.

As we sneaked up, how strange the little encampment looked,

ME WITH OUR COLLIE, LADDIE, 1931.

illuminated by wavering, weak flashlights. Alternately sinister and romantic, they were gypsies or vagabonds. But mostly I retained the tone of ridicule borrowed from the aunts: What sort of people would make such a fuss over a berry nobody thought good enough to eat?

Three of the Milfs family were crouched over the tarpaulin and sheets as if hunting for something they had lost and couldn't quite find. The ground covering seemed to domesticate the scene. Mr. Milfs held the steadiest flashlight, talking all the while to Jack, who wasn't participating in the harvest. The Milfs boy in the tree would get a purchase on a limb and ride it violently, causing a hail of berries. Then Mrs. Milfs and the girl, helped by the older boys from our family, would fall upon the booty, scoop it up, and fill the receptacles.

When my companion and I arrived, nobody paid us any attention. We helped rake in the berries, which squished easily in one's fingers. I noted the mess of twigs and leaves accompanying the fruit we gathered and wondered what use Mrs. Milfs could make of any of this.

"All right, stand back," Milf Milfs said gravely. He lurched a little, his legs cramped from scrambling around on the drop cloths. In the moonlight Mrs. Milfs looked pleased and carefully sheltered the bowls of dark berries from an accidental upset.

The Milfs boy in the tree continued to shake, now in vicious jerks, like a terrier killing a rat. A new patter of berries fell upon the outstretched coverings, plus a rustle of fruit falling in the grass beyond the drop cloths, never to be found or gathered. Mrs. Milfs was aware of this waste and unhappy over the berries missed because they didn't have a wide enough net. She told her son not to shake so hard.

Then to us gleaners: "Let's pick up each corner. It'll go faster that way." As we did so, the berries rolled together like mercury on the loose.

"No, no; we should be sorting first," said the nine-year-old Milfs girl, pushing back her blonde pigtails. "We're gettin' too much junk."

Mother and daughter argued a bit over this, until Milf sided with the girl. Then we all bent to hand-sort, while Jack stood talking, asking about Milf's work load in the foundry, wondering if he could get a broken sprocket fixed real quick should he need it by tomorrow, since thrashing would soon begin. But Milfs didn't wish to go into shop matters; he said nothing. Jack bragged about how professionally he had soldered a pipe with his new blowtorch. He sought to have his machinist skills confirmed by someone outside our family. Then he complimented them on the amount of mulberries they had gathered, figuring they must surely be through, for all the pans and bowls were full.

"Let's move over to those trees on the left," said Milf. We all obeyed, the Milfs boy down and up the trees with simian quickness, while we helped spread coverings in the new location.

Mrs. Milfs removed her apron, which would now serve as a bag for the fruit, though the stains would be nearly impossible to get out in next Monday's wash. A straw hat and cap were also put to use as containers.

"Curtis, run to the house," said Jack, "there're some empty cans on the back porch."

"No, no, we'll manage fine," Mrs. Milfs insisted. "Once we get to the car, there's an oilcloth. We'll dump them in that."

Jack clearly thought the Milfses were overdoing it but tried to make them at ease in their greed. "Plenty of mulberries out here; take whatever you want. Might as well; only the birds would get 'em, since we sure don't want any ourselves."

"Why, they're perfectly good!"

I was tiring of the work. It would be more fun to tell the homefolks on the porch just what was going on out here.

I hurried while my news from the front was fresh—spilling it out upon arrival at the top of my voice: "They've got *tubs* of berries! Pots and pans full; bushels and bushels of mulberries!"

"My, that's really good," said Lizzie, an edge of dubiousness clouding her statement. "I'm sure they don't have a chance at anything like it in town."

Out here, lots of food for the picking: from trees, shrubs, bushes, scattered on the ground, or under it. We were of the earth and full of our connection to it, nourished by the land's surprising bountifulness, whereas those in cities had no such shorings to their lives, no certainty of sustenance.

"Why so many berries?" Bertha wondered.

"And to come at night!" said Elizabeth.

"You know Milf works late, especially now in summer," Lizzie commented. "You have a breakdown, it better be fixed quick, or you could lose a field."

"They had to finish supper, get cleaned up," Mother added. In the city (Remsen with its population of 1,200 qualified as such) folks didn't pay all that much attention to nightfall. It wasn't the marking it was for us. The sun's going down for them meant no more than time to turn on the lights.

"If we'd *sold* 'em the mulberries, we could've made a lot."

"You only sell things you want yourself, that are valuable," Mother reminded me. "If we had lots of raspberries, we might consider selling *them*." But there never were enough. She appended a homily about remembering the less fortunate, who didn't have the variety of fruit available to us. Clearly she did not approve of the condescension in the air. If the Milfses thought mulberries tasted as good as blackberries and were happy with them, just as well.

When the mulberry pickers bearing their haul finally returned to the car, Mother and Lizzie walked out to greet them. Milf Milfs carefully placed the berries in the back seat, then opened the trunk to stash more of them away. With the doors open and the dome light shining, the fruit looked lustrous and tempting. Mother and Lizzie oohed and aahed, while Jack scrutinized the front end of the Ford, saying the wheels looked a little out of alignment. The earth's abundance he took for granted—it was more or less his burden, incessantly needing attention. He loved that other world of machines, which were man-made and capable of being controlled.

"My, what a lot you got!" Mother exclaimed, and Mrs. Milfs returned a shy, proud smile. "Such nice big ones, too."

"We certainly do thank you," she murmured, looking back and forth to Lizzie and Mother, whose okay verified Jack's original invitation, since they were responsible for the family's food.

"Why, we're so glad you can use them," said Lizzie, trying to breach the embarrassment caused by this exposure of the difference between the haves and have-nots.

Mrs. Milfs hung her head a little to one side. "I hear . . . you never bother with mulberries." Was it an accusation? Or a way of getting on an equal footing with us?

"Aren't they nice!" Mother reached a hand in toward a brimful bowl. "We had lots of rain this year; it's made 'em so juicy. Can I have one?"

I was surprised and watched carefully.

Mrs. Milfs smiled uncertainly.

"Any one?"

"Go ahead. We've plenty."

Mother selected the biggest, most luscious berry in the largest bowl. Lizzie did the same, deliberately searching for the very best mulberry she could find. Then I did the same, and so did my siblings—at least two of them—who'd come up behind me. Lizzie held the mulberry by its green stem as if afraid the tender flesh of the fruit might break should she touch it with her finger. Then she plopped it into her mouth, stem and all, chewing with an expression of fake delight. "Wonderful!"

"Yes, really quite good," Mother said, swallowing.

The sickish-tasting fruit turned my stomach, but I stopped myself from spitting it out.

"Go on. Help yourself to more," said Mrs. Milfs in a funny, almost defiant voice. But Milf Milfs slammed the doors, which turned off the dome light, and started the motor.

Mrs. Milfs extended her hand to touch Lizzie's freckled arm. "Thank you so much. You're awfully good to us."

Were we?

"Why, come back—if you need more. Long as they last."

Jack repeated Lizzie's invitation in different words—generosity spilling out. "Though, can't say many mulberries are left after the job you folks done." Then he seemed to catch himself, hoping he hadn't given offense by implying that the Milfs family had cleaned us out (which they pretty much had). "Where's the boy? Didn't leave him up a tree, did you?" He poked his head into the back seat area and put his hand on the squirming youngster next to the bowls. "Oh, there you are! Not going to spend the night in the trees?"

We all waved as the car pulled away.

In the moment of emptiness after their departure—which seemed a letdown—Jack said to Lizzie: "Milf wondered if he could pick field corn for eating when it comes in."

"Sure, why not?" But her voice sounded a little closed in, and I wondered, too, how far these people would go if you just let them keep coming out.

"I told him I'd let him know when the milk is in the kernels."

"They probably didn't plant sweet corn—in their garden in

THE SEVEN OF US, 1932. BACK ROW (left to right): ME, KENNETH, ROBERT, DONALD, LLOYD. FRONT ROW: RUTH, LOIS.

town," Mother said.

"No room for *that*," Jack agreed.

"Field corn? What we feed the pigs?"

"In the blister stage it's real good," Mother told me. "Before sweet corn was developed, everybody ate field corn. It's edible only a few days. You have to catch it just right. When we were young, we didn't have sweet corn, did we Lizzie?"

"I guess not. A person forgets."

We turned back to the porch and the lemonade about to be served. Lizzie had long ago decided there was only enough of the drink for the family.

First they took mulberries; next the corn. Others would come for our wild grapes to make juice and jelly; hunt rabbits and squirrels in our grove for their stews; and some neighbors would make off with our wood in order to keep warm in winter if they couldn't afford coal or their pile of corncobs had run out.

Always there would be more than we could ever use—here afloat in bountifulness—while beyond our farm the money had stopped, the banks were failing. A world of want existed, but Lord, how much we had.

BULLETINS

Soon after establishing the prairie homestead, Grandfather made use of his carpentry skills by helping to
build a white frame church. A mellow-sounding bell,
which had been forged in an eastern Iowa foundry, was
set in the belfry. But by the late 1930s our minister talked of
replacing the edifice with a new house of worship because at present
there was no basement room for Ladies Aid meetings and Sunday
School classes; no place for bridal showers or receptions after
funerals or weddings; and no nook for mothers with crying babies

ME (on the right) WITH REVEREND
AND THE CONFIRMATION CLASS OF 1940,
CHRIST LUTHERAN CHURCH, REMSEN.

to seclude themselves yet listen to the sermon over a sound system.

Reverend was not a modern clergyman except for this publicly announced goal: to have a new brick church. According to synod literature, such campaigns renewed the parishioners' commitment to religion. These efforts were needed periodically, the draw upon the purse having the effect of bringing fresh attention to God's word proclaimed from the pulpit. A strangely inappropriate alliance perhaps, but that's how religion worked: always a connection between giving money and being saved, though never put in those terms.

To us, however, the proposed brick church, Spanish mission in style (odd for these parts), would just not seem ours. There would be no steeple, only a small belfry on the side, where hymn tunes in chimes might be broadcast to the whole town and countryside on Sunday mornings.

A church without a bell? Whoever heard of such a thing! All these decades Grandpa's bell with its beautiful, deep tone had tolled the years on the occasion of a death in the congregation. I had pulled the coarse rope to make it clang just before Sunday services when I became an usher at age thirteen, after being confirmed as a bona fide member of the church. Uncle Jack was particularly upset that the architectural plans did not include reinstallation of the bell, and he was horrified at the cost of the building—totally inappropriate for wartime. Army veteran that he was, any lack of instant patriotism which he might observe in the community "got his goat." The church building effort, launched at the start of the forties, would appropriate vital materials needed for the national emergency. All four boys in his family would be joining up when the time came for them to do so, whereas in other farm families many sons received 2-C deferments; an easy way out, because of their employment in the crucial industry of agriculture.

When the church building committee came to Jack for a donation, he asked if that request wasn't in conflict with the federal government's war bond drives? How would anybody around here know there was a war on? Perhaps they might be a little inconvenienced by ration-book coupons for gasoline and sugar, but even these restrictions were easily circumvented by unlimited fuel allowances for tractors—which could be tapped for any farmer's auto as well. And extra sugar coupons for preserving fruit could be wheedled out of the local Office of Price Administration.

Some said the old bell ought to be contributed to a scrap iron drive, but Jack hated the thought of such a fate for it, knowing how much discarded iron most farmers still had lying around in the weeds. And there were those in the congregation who thought the belfry might one day be enlarged to accommodate it after folks tired of the novelty of chimes. So the bell ended up in the center of town. Whenever somebody bought enough war bonds to make a noise about it, they rang the old bell. Jack said it pained him to hear that ringing, for it only emphasized his difficulty: his loyalties pulled in opposite directions, between church and country.

All the while, the Missouri Synod Lutheranism proclaimed by Reverend with relentless conviction successfully took hold in me, almost without my knowing it. Reverend was a strong presence in our lives, though physically not very prepossessing: fairly short and slim, with a button nose and somewhat bulbous eyes, a mouth too full and flannely for the narrow jaw; dark hair that went straight up to add to his height but which reminded me of the china heads you plant with seeds for green hair to grow. Since Reverend's name ended in the same *ck* letters as mine, I figured his people and ours (on father's side) originated from the same section of Germany, near Rostock on the Baltic Sea, probably emigrating from the port of Hamburg about when Greatgrandfather did in the mid-nineteenth century.

In his somber black ministerial robe, Reverend took his pastoral mission as seriously as those centuries of Lutheran ministers under the louring skies of northern Europe. Reverend thoroughly believed that he represented God the Father, a spiritual backup to our terrestrial fathers; he insisted we listen and obey or punishment would be severe in the afterlife. Each and every one of his sermons bore the essential message that we were damned to hell but might be saved through the blood of Jesus Christ, provided we believe. The message, delivered with ominous theatrics, always came with the warning that repentance tomorrow might be too late and we would end up tortured in eternal flames.

Proficient in German, Reverend delivered a sermon in that language once a month before regular services began. However, as the pioneer members died off and the war with Hitler began, the services in *Deutsch* were discontinued and never held in the new brick church.

Our fresh religious quarters sparked a hope in the younger ones that Reverend might bend a little and be more modern. Though such a softening was not in his nature, perhaps he realized he was expected to try. We younger members clamored for a youth organization,

REVEREND LAYING THE CORNERSTONE
OF THE NEW CHURCH, 1942. UNCLE
JACK, WEARING A DARK SUIT,
IS IN THE CENTER.

which our parents encouraged, figuring it might keep us from slipping off and marrying Catholics. But to Reverend, the fact that a few young ministers in the synod prided themselves on their casual, back-slapping relationship with parishioners might only indicate a lapse in pastoral leadership. Shouldn't the Lutheran minister always dwell a little apart and not be as others were? Not socialize in town, avidly follow sports, engage in small talk, or pursue hobbies publicly. God the Father should be his sole preoccupation.

Perhaps Reverend hoped the new edifice might be novelty enough to squelch their ideas regarding religious easement, but the times were moving away from any dominie's hold on a congregation. Reverend couldn't change his menacing pulpit style; it wasn't in him. Now with the handsome building, a few more communicants were added to the church lists, but grumblings and complaints about Reverend seemed to grow, each family having a different set of grievances—some privately held and never openly expressed.

Of course we eventually became used to the church and also contributed to its furnishings. Jack gave the United States flag on a standard, flanking one side of the altar; Mother, the ecclesiastical flag in memory of Father, on the other; and Aunt Bertha and Grandma paid for gold vases placed at the feet of the statue of Jesus—receptacles that nicely set off the summer flowers from Bertha's garden.

In the brick house of worship, fancier elements came into play, as if we had moved up in the religious world: a visitor's book on a pedestal in the narthex; young ushers (often me) to escort parishioners to available spaces, Reverend having urged us to see that the front pews were filled up. We handed each churchgoer a *Bulletin,* a folded sheet containing the order of service and news items the pastor wished to convey.

Concordia Publishers in St. Louis printed the *Bulletin,* using a religious motif on the front fold such as Jesus in the temple showing off his learning before the elders, radiant light surrounding his clean-cut, un-Semitic face. The back flap advertised various religious books available from the printer. Reverend typed the inside contents each week and ran the *Bulletin* off on his mimeograph machine. In the old church the congregation had scrutinized the signboard up in front to see what hymn to sing, though they usually knew from habit when the Nicene Creed was to be spoken in unison and when the Lord's

Prayer came. After a collection-plate offering prayer at the altar, Reverend would slowly turn around, clear his throat, try to muster a secular smile, and in a low-key voice announce meetings or inform us who was to be married, buried, or baptized.

Now all of this church news appeared in the *Bulletin*. After services it was carried home tucked in personal hymn books (our names stamped in gold on the cover), because to leave it behind would seem disrespectful. The following Sunday as you picked up the hymnal and started off to church, the old *Bulletin* was laid aside. A small stack of these grew on top of the bookcase at the bottom of the stairs. Eventually Carrie or Lizzie would take the *Bulletins* up to the attic, for it would seem sacrilegious to burn them in the trash barrel, where other paper goods ended up. Concordia's Jesus stared out at one too severely for that.

So here in the attic they all are. As I pick through them, church days and a good many of those parishioners return vividly. Somewhere among the stack I might even find the one with Reverend's untimely news item on brother Robert, which had so upset Mother. We had just learned of his collapse on a New Guinea battlefield and subsequent airlift to a California military hospital. However, since we didn't know exactly what his situation was and cousins Hazel or Della or other family members who lived in California hadn't yet been to visit him, it was too soon to have to explain anything to people. But the Lutheran chaplain in the Army hospital notified Reverend, who put it in print—and we felt our privacy had been invaded.

Sometimes I wondered if those weekly *Bulletins* fulfilled the minister's secret craving to be a journalist—not so much to report the news as to give it a sane, Christian perspective. Perhaps we should have made more of an effort to believe him. With his list of noteworthy items, accompanied by a homily, he was enclosing our small world of Christ Lutheran Church in order to make us into a pastoral family. The trouble was, the news as found in the *Bulletin* did not jibe all that well with the rest of our lives. In any small town there is the steamy "undernews," about which everyone hears, as well as the public news, safe enough to appear in the weekly *Bell-Enterprise;* and then there was this church version.

Despite Reverend's pulpit declarations regarding the wickedness inherent in all humankind, he was naive about the ways of the community, partly because he did not function at all outside the church. A daily walk to and from the post office was the extent of his acquaintance with the town. The *Bulletin* announcements kept revealing how little he knew about us.

For instance, one year the local public high school hired an exceptionally talented basketball coach, much liked by everyone. His prim, quiet wife wore her hair in tightly coiled rolls; she attended our church quite regularly with their three children, though he did not. As in other little Iowa burgs, the girls' basketball team was more important than the boys', and Remsen's chances looked good for a strong showing in the spring state basketball tournament. The girls won almost every game of their regular season, partly because of an outstanding player whom I'll call Trudy Mueller, who shot most of the baskets and was said to have the coach "wrapped around her little finger." What made girls' basketball fun were the emotional outbursts and extreme excitement of the players—all of which tickled the fans, who were themselves stolid, quiet, and seldom given to such eruptions. If Trudy happened to miss a lay-up shot, she would throw herself upon the coach's shoulder and bewail her failure—somewhat to his embarrassment, since the crowd in the bleachers was watching and smiling over the way he was blushing.

To make the team this good, the coach had the girls practicing every weeknight until quite late, though the Muellers were grateful they didn't have to drive in from the farm to fetch Trudy. The coach delivered her home himself, no matter what the weather. All that winter the patrons of cafes and beer joints praised the coach for how good he was with girls, the way he could key them up or calm them down.

But just when the play-offs began, Trudy was sidelined; the team went down in defeat. Such a disappointment! What could be wrong with the girl? She told her parents she was no doubt pregnant, having missed a couple of her periods. Seems the coach had not been taking her straight home after practice but would often park with her somewhere. It had been going on for months. Quickly an illegal abortion was arranged for Trudy in Kansas City. Since she would be missing choir practice for several weeks, as well as other church activities, the Muellers informed Reverend that she would be away to have a "special operation." He put the news in the *Bulletin* and urged all to send her get-well cards.

Reverend's unworldliness was typical of ministers and their wives in those days. The writer Ruth Suckow, born to a clergyman's family, tells in *Some Others and Myself* about their Sunday School superintendent, who got into a drunken brawl and was badly beaten up, but "my innocent mother . . . asked that the school send its affectionate greetings 'to our superintendent, who is kept at home by illness.'"

Catholics, meanwhile, seemed to illustrate how to be at ease in life. They kept the Remsen taverns open even on Sunday morning so that they could drink a few shots after Mass, ignoring Iowa's Prohibition laws. Descendants of Luxemburgers and south Germans, their cultural imprint was quite different from ours, and the two camps were often at odds. They indulged in various forms of unlawful gambling—including cockfights—and played cards for high stakes. Our side saw the Catholics—with no birth control, only the rhythm method—rapidly multiplying, whereas our ranks were diminishing. One classmate of mine would have fifteen children. The nurses at St. Joseph's hospital sent her home with "We'll see you next year!"

Remsen's public school, where I attended seventh and eighth grades, had only about a dozen in each class, often less. Local Catholics grumbled about paying school taxes in order to maintain such a small operation, particularly since the priest insisted they send their own kids to the huge parochial school, badly overcrowded—and of course tuition was charged. Cooperative ventures between the schools in music teaching and manual training did little to alleviate the situation. There was even a proposal to buy the public school building, use it as an annex to the parochial school across the street, and bus the Protestant scholars elsewhere. That scheme was "going altogether too far," Lutherans felt, and their indignation mounted.

Next, some Catholics proposed buying a bus with public school funds but having it service the parochial pupils as well. Surely there were laws against that! Suggestions of this sort increased the tension; rumors spread. The priest was supposedly making the rounds of his businessmen, telling the storekeepers not to hire Protestant help; one boy was believed to have been fired as a result. This same priest was seen hanging around the grain wagons in threshing time, getting pledges for the school building fund as the crop came in.

Reactions were loud and angry. The other Protestant preacher in town, at St. Paul's Evangelical, across the street from our church, delivered a baccalaureate address with ringing indignation. He said our servicemen had fought the war to keep church and state separate and to guarantee free education, among other things, and those in Remsen who were threatening these principles should be thrown to the bottom of the sea and stay down there with all the other slimy things.

Aunts Bertha and Elizabeth were also highly agitated. They drove off to a remote rural schoolhouse in the western part of the county, where a defrocked priest held forth, exposing the machinations and corruptions of the Roman church.

Even Reverend rose to the occasion in this crisis. While conducting confirmation instruction for maturing youngsters in the front pews of the church before regular services began, he proclaimed in a loud voice that the Catholic religion was gravely at fault in Christian doctrine and beliefs. He also stated in the *Bulletin* that interested parishioners should arrive early to hear what he had to say on the subject.

Then the wife of our Lutheran grocer spread the news that her husband's partner, a young Catholic whom he had taken in and trusted, had been embezzling for years and now owned the building—in fact, he was in a position to take over the business. Although a lawyer advised that perhaps a case could be made if there were more hard evidence, the shocked grocer quietly sold out his interest and took a clerical job in a rival store. In time he and his wife, who was still fulminating, moved to California, where emancipated Iowans are fond of going in order to make over their lives—and where the "Catholic menace" is less evident.

Those who stayed had no choice but to fight; and some of us Lutherans won, among them my classmate Donnie. After a stint in the army, he returned to Remsen and fell in love with a Catholic girl, Joan. They decided to marry, but no, he would not convert; *she* would have to come over to our side.

In the early stages of the courtship, Donnie drove Joan to Sioux City, where the motion picture *Martin Luther* was playing at the Orpheum, telling her the film would surely be an eye-opener for her. Afterward, she admitted never having been aware of this version of those momentous events at Wittenberg in the sixteenth century; she had instead believed Luther to be an aberrant priest, a troublemaker who wanted to marry and, therefore, tried to justify leaving the Church. Donnie happily engineered her religious re-education, finally enrolling her in Reverend's Bible-study class for those about to be confirmed.

News of their engagement became the talk of the community. Donnie refused to confer with the local priest, but upon Joan's insistence he did see a Roman clergyman in a neighboring town to discuss the personal impact of their forthcoming alliance. Donnie was flatly informed that if Joan broke with the Church, she would be damned to hell. "You show me in the Bible where it says she'll be damned to hell if she leaves the Catholic Church!" he replied. Then the priest handed him papers to sign pertaining to the upbringing of children in a mixed marriage. Donnie threw them on the floor. "I don't want any of this. You won't see *me* signing. I've already got plenty of these forms laying around at home."

As a post office employee, Donnie was in a perfect position to spread the word as needed—and he was never the silent type. Way back when we were both in knickers, Donnie stood at the lively center of whatever devilry we might be up to, especially at Sunday School picnics.

While talking to Joan's father, Donnie happened to mention God—for the Deity seemed to be playing a huge part in his life of late. "Oh, I'm tired hearing about that God of yours," Joan's father said. To which Donnie replied: "Well, who do *you* pray to, may I ask? Don't we all pray to God? Or do you say your prayers to a little old man who sits in Rome?"

Hearing this account in the post office one morning, a Catholic shook his head at Donnie and smiled. "You Lutherans know more about your religion than we do about ours. We only do what the priests say. Don't know why or what it's all about; just do as they say."

Donnie and Joan's religion-crossed love even became an international cause célèbre. After the war, food parcels were sent to needy German families through the contacts of Remsen relatives. A Bavarian priest was one of the recipients; he was a pen pal of a local woman who scribbled the news of the unfortunate romance that held everyone's attention. In his reply he expressed his concern, reassuring her that he would say a special prayer at Mass for the salvation of

Joan in her ordeal.

The last weeks before the wedding the controversy raged so bitterly that Joan became afraid to stay in her apartment over the Gambles store. Donnie's mother solved that problem by taking her in.

The shower for the engaged couple, in our new church basement, was attended by over one hundred; the gifts were stacked almost to the ceiling. Donnie's sisters-in-law presided. Two little girls did a tap dance number and the best choir singer rendered "The Lord's Prayer." A lunch of ham on dark and egg on white was served, with coffee, jello, and cake. Although the priest ordered that no Catholics attend the shower or wedding, many delighted in disobeying the dictum.

Donnie undid each elaborately wrapped package down to the box, then handed it to Joan. After all the gifts had been opened, Joan rose from her place to thank everyone. "You know where we'll be living—there above the Gambles store. I want you *all* to come visit us." Then she was overwhelmed by tears and several nearby women rushed forward to embrace her. Now she belonged to us.

But eventually both sides began to tire of the religious tension and back-and-forth fighting. Ecumenical efforts were stirring throughout the world, and Christianity as a whole seemed too threatened by secularism of various sorts to survive such petty quarreling. The new priest in Remsen had a less militant outlook, and our Reverend seemed about to retire.

Lately he'd been making more gaffes than usual, managing to offend in small, irritating ways. For example, Jack became upset over yet another *Bulletin.* One Sunday in late November near the birthdays of his dead sons, Lloyd and Donald, Jack happened to mark his collection-plate envelope with their names, by way of private remembrance. Next week he found his contribution listed "In memory of his loving sons, John Harnack gives three dollars." —"Made me look like such a cheapskate!" Jack grumbled.

Reverend's clumsiness also irritated aunts Elizabeth and Anne. Aunt Anne was home on leave from her restaurant job to care for Bertha, who was fatally ill with cancer. Anne and Elizabeth had been trying to remain staunchly supportive of the church, particularly because of the Catholic threat, but even they had about had enough. The breaking point came when my grandmother died at age 92 while

Bertha was in the hospital recovering from an operation. Because of her weak condition, Elizabeth and Anne didn't want her to know of their mother's death at this time. But Reverend sent Bertha a condolence card "with little wilted flowers on it," which somehow had to be explained. When my aunts scolded Reverend for what he had done, he tried to make amends, but Elizabeth insisted to us, "He didn't apologize enough."

After Bertha's death the two remaining sisters decided to give the church a pair of candlesticks in her memory. Reverend proceeded to order them from an ecclesiastical supplier, and he scheduled the dedication for a Sunday in June, placing the announcement in the *Bulletin* on that day but inadvertently forgetting to notify Elizabeth and Anne beforehand. Perhaps he figured those two never missed a Sunday, so it really didn't matter. But the Greiman family reunion in eastern Iowa—Grandma's people—was usually held the third Sunday in June. No doubt Elizabeth and Anne felt a particular need after the loss of Bertha and their mother to renew lifelong bonds of kinship with their many cousins; so they were out of town when the candlesticks were dedicated. As Anne later put it, "A terrible thing has happened." The memorial to Bertha took place without them being present to witness it. Nor did anyone place cut flowers from Bertha's garden around the altar; maintaining Bertha's extensive floral plantings was a pledge to her memory they both had made.

For weeks afterward my aunts could not bring themselves to enter the church. Anne said she would cry if she saw those candlesticks on the altar and remembered what Reverend had done. Therefore, each Sunday they became transient worshippers, visiting other Lutheran churches in the area, listening to different preachers—for although they were on the outs with Reverend, they were still on God's side.

One consolation to Jack during these waning years of Reverend's tenure was that the chimes didn't work out, just as he had foretold. When at last they were functioning properly, no organist could do justice to them. Nor could they be played except on Sunday morning, whereas a bell was useful anytime. The old custom of tolling the years after someone died seemed worthy of being reinstated. Of course, the families who had contributed to the chimes through memorial bequests were unhappy about this development. Now there was talk of enlarging the belfry and putting Grandpa's bell back into Christ Lutheran Church—if it could be found. Our family readily agreed to underwrite the cost of this: a bell fund in memory of Grandma. Elizabeth and Anne, delighted by the fitness of such a memorial, spoke of trying to get all of us kids to come home at the same time, so that we could attend service together.

Up front near the altar, banks of Bertha's flowers would be splendidly arrayed. And Reverend would have placed a note in the *Bulletin* that we had provided funds for the installation of the bell. We would be sitting in the first pews, and everyone would know the Harnacks were having their own family commemoration. *That* would make up for all the wrongs of recent years in this church.

But just about then, Reverend retired.

Perhaps it was indeed time that he took himself off the scene, but why had he kept his intentions so secret? Probably he couldn't figure out a way of telling the elders that he now could afford to, after crying poor so long. Certainly his stipend was unconscionably meager, the parsonage rather bleak and underfurnished. "If you want to see a period piece, come over to the parsonage and look at the wallpaper in an upstairs bedroom," he once told the church fathers. "Hasn't been papered in eighteen or twenty years." Although Jack brought Reverend and his wife a dozen or more eggs on a weekly basis, it was viewed not as income supplement, but a special treat of "farm freshness" for these city dwellers.

Rumors had long held that Reverend's wife was a woman of means and perhaps owned a couple of farms. Certainly the pastor's car was always quite new, his two children well-dressed, and both went to a Missouri Synod Lutheran college; the money was coming from somewhere other than his salary. Gossips figured that the couple would probably retire in the town from which Reverend's wife hailed, less than twenty miles away. So some of them drove there, looked around for new house-building, found a good-sized structure, and asked the workmen who it was for. Hit the mark, the first try.

My, what a big place! So many rooms—what would they need them for, now with the children gone? She must have inherited several farms, in addition to what she already had.

A new grudging, money-respect replaced their former view of the preacher and his wife; awe over Reverend's hellfire and damnation now gave way to admiration of earthly treasures laid up. They suspected Reverend had not announced his plans because the lavish scale of the proposed retirement would have unsettled parishioners. Should a minister, even a retired one, live so well? Would it reflect adversely on the message he'd been conveying—eye of the needle and all that?

Suddenly the pastor and his wife were about to leave. A few rushed farewell get-togethers were held, then the parsonage stood empty. A call went out through the synod, and before long a young fellow in robes moved around in front of the altar on Sundays like an imposter, speaking religious profundities that seemed out of keeping with how callow he looked. Great with young people, a real regular guy, fond of sports, active in community affairs. It was refreshing at first, though startling. Did such a style go with God? In the pulpit he couldn't scare anybody into paying really close attention. The pipeline to the Almighty didn't seem to be there anymore—but where was it, anyhow? Difficult, terrible periods occurred in everyone's life when you had to roust up the old beliefs in order to get through. Now no little fierce-eyed man in a black gown held everything in place the way it had once been.

The new minister didn't last; another came. By that time I was mostly away at college. I never transferred my church membership or was released from Christ Lutheran to some other parish. I had had quite enough of the institutional aspects of religion. Perhaps something in my genes—generations of family church-involvement going back to Germany—kept me still believing in a divine presence of sorts, though not to be worshipped in concert with others; it became too private a matter even to be discussed with loved ones. If it was true that Adolph von Harnack had been a distant cousin of Grandfather's, as genealogical buffs in our clan maintained, then our family had long since paid its religious dues. Harnack, a professor of religion at the University of Berlin, was largely responsible for helping to reconcile Darwinism with the Bible, thereby saving the Christian faith.

My problem was, I desperately needed to be saved from the punishing brand of religion I'd been raised on. In our family the ethics were sound, morals clean; we needed no such pummeling from the pulpit. In fact, we tended to be too good for the sake of our mental and physical health. Instead of being sinners who should repent wicked ways, we needed to sin a bit and commit ourselves to sloth at least now and then. As every Catholic knows, if the Church grabs you while young, it has you for life. Much the same was true for me; I faced a long struggle to free myself from Lutheran fundamentalism.

The first dogma I renounced was the notion that in Adam's fall we sinned all and embraced instead the doctrine of human perfectibility—including the notion that even one's bodily desires were in the approved scheme of things and might not be considered all that bad. I tried to accept the precepts of a transcendentalist movement called "New Thought," which involved guiding one's emotions and controlling the mind's impulses. I meditated, first learning how to relax my body joint by joint, starting from the toes, then filling my head with "spirit," which was supposed to happen (by means of a mantra I chanted to myself) after all thoughts were erased. For a while it seemed to work, but I could never remember to follow the procedure on a regular basis.

Still, the biggest obstacle wasn't a religious hang-up, per se, but repressed sexuality from which it partly stemmed. I envied the Catholics their supposed lack of inhibitions in this department. Luckily as I matured the girls said I had "bedroom eyes" and thought me good-looking, would summon me into the closet for a special delivery in our junior high games of Post Office, or settle under a bush with me in Five Minutes of Heaven, when according to the rules there were no rules—at least for five minutes. However, full sexual activity for me would take some doing, partly because of the strictures upon "good girls" to hold out and save themselves for marriage. They were told that all boys—even nice ones like me—were only after that "one thing." Which was true enough.

Not surprisingly, I was still a virgin when I joined the Navy just before my eighteenth birthday. After boot camp at Great Lakes, I was assigned to Naval facilities in Chicago. By that time I knew that my initiation would not come about through a Clark Street lady of the night or a streetwalker hanging around the entrance of the Chicago Servicemen's Center. Reverend had long ago rendered me impotent for such unsavory shenanigans.

Trim in my sailor's uniform—though I couldn't offer the drama of perhaps being shipped out soon (the war was over)—at last I was making romantic time with a delightful, buxom nurse in training at Chicago's St. Luke's hospital. We had been introduced by a Le Mars high school classmate, who was also in residence there. Because of her profession, I figured she would be thoroughly familiar with all male bodily territories and even should I falter (heaven forbid!) once things progressed that far, would know precisely what to do.

For weeks, however, our frenzied necking sessions had most of the characteristics of all that I had already been through with many good girls back home. The "passion pit" crannies in the lounge of the hospital dormitory were scenes of prolonged heavy petting by couples like us but clearly they weren't the place for anything more. How could I manage it with her—where? Luckily, her folks didn't live too far away, in a western suburb easily reached by train; perhaps we might spend a weekend together out there soon, I suggested. She agreed, indicating we'd probably pretty much have the run of the place, since her mother was busy with charities and her father had a lot of church duties—he was a Congregational minister.

Rather gave me a turn to find that out! Would I never be free of the fell hand of the clergy? Congregationalism, though, was liberal and open-minded, as I knew from chapel at Grinnell College; still, my expectations were subdued as we rode the train out. Around the dinner table that evening conversation flowed easily, her jovial, kindly parents relaxed about me keeping their daughter company. I kept studying this minister, for there seemed little that was preacherly about him. Then shortly after rising from the table, they bade us farewell, claiming an engagement for the evening. Could it be their daughter had prearranged this strategy in order to allow us courting privacy? We had the house to ourselves, and I could hardly contain my eagerness to grab her, though first we washed up the supper dishes, being good children.

After thrashing around on the living room sofa, which seemed too close to the front window, we moved into her father's den and bedded down on a scratchy horsehair davenport, scarcely missing a beat in our groping amours, our tongued kisses. The abrasive upholstery discouraged a flesh-on-flesh development, however, and the boxy davenport confined us like the back seat of a car. But soon her essential garments were mostly out of the way, and the thirteen buttons on my sailor pants front flap were all undone, one for each of the original states of the Union. Her eyes were rolled back, with only the whites showing, which told me she must be ready.

But I was having technical difficulties, not knowing much about what I was doing, yet in such a state of near orgasm that I knew I'd better roll on that protection, which I kept in a foil in my wallet. Upon rearing back I knocked over a huge Bible on a stand nearby. It fell partially on top of us, sending me over the edge, while she cried out. Then we both laughed, recovered, and straightened things up a bit. Luckily we did, for the minister and his wife returned unexpectedly early, headlights swinging into the driveway and flashing up along the ceiling.

Somehow in later weeks there never was an opportunity for us to complete what had been so rudely interrupted by Holy Writ. And I could only regard the intimacy we had shared as not counting for much, since there had been little in it for her. One way or another it seemed the Bible kept coming down on my backside; but sexuality would eventually be the winner, even as it had been for Martin Luther and his nun wife.

The scene shifts to some years later, a walk-up apartment on West 104th Street in New York. There the girl I am seeing lives in a room rented from Alice, whose little boy may or may not be the illegitimate son of the middle-aged man bearing a famous New York society name who is a gentleman caller just like me on Saturday nights. Only, I always left the apartment after a few hours of lovemaking. Residual sin anxieties kept shoving me out of that warm bed which I'd been enjoying—down into the streets and back up Broadway to my Columbia dormitory room, usually at some ungodly hour after midnight.

Why, why must you always leave? my hurt girlfriend kept asking, feeling the affront. I couldn't really explain, hardly knowing the answer myself. But perhaps she guessed what was behind my determined escapes. Earlier she had watched me carefully prop a chair under the doorknob, so that nobody could barge in while we were in the throes of our passion—though the door was already locked and bolted, as she pointed out. No way the little boy or anyone else could sneak in here and spy on us while we made love. Still, I could not shake a fear of being "caught"; couldn't explain the power of the guilt driving me from Eden and Reverend's residual force. Locks and doors were no barriers when it came to withstanding the sinner's guilty conscience.

And so it was; the tilted chair under the doorknob did not stop Reverend. One night after exceptionally vigorous lovemaking, I shuddered out of a deep sleep, caught in a nightmarish fit of terror,

ME UNDER THE EL NEAR COLUMBIA UNIVERSITY,
NEW YORK, 1949.

and reared up from the sleeping naked body next to me, uttering a gasp of alarm. In the vivid dream which still held me, Reverend had come through the door, his billowing sable sleeves uplifted, a vindictive, admonishing look in his eye.

Yes, my pounding heart gradually subsided as she stroked me calm and talked to me quietly; and yes I was young, easily aroused, and we were soon eager for each other once again. That evening for the first time, I spent the night.

BERTHA'S TIME

Under the eaves, where as children Lois and I never penetrated, we now find early rural school readers and exercise books, German language children's tales, a set of etched fingerbowls, a broken double-globed kerosene lamp of the kind antique dealers call "Gone With the Wind," and two diaries by my father's sisters: Elizabeth's covers her first year at Cedar Falls Normal School in 1907; Bertha's records the year 1913, when she turns twenty-seven. I tuck them in a pocket for careful perusal later.

Bertha's diary was perhaps undertaken as a New Year's resolution. The lined notepad surely wasn't a Christmas gift, for it's an ordinary sort, available in any notions store of the time. She would set herself the task of jotting down remarks about each day, to see if she could, and to test her powers of determination, her character. Making faithful entries would prove her mettle, at least to herself. Nobody was expected to read it, and she herself forgot the diary in her move to town with her parents seven years later.

"Happy New Year 1913," she begins, and certainly it starts off that way, with cousins Herman and Will Katter as houseguests and Elizabeth home for the holidays from teaching. "Have potatoes, roast goose, dressing, citron pickles, peas, apple and banana salad, tapioca pudding. Sit in front room and talk, later take Kodak pictures. Then make ice cream. Dress and get things ready for our evening party. Have a crowd of thirty-five." They play Show and Blindman's Bluff and finish by eating "chicken sandwiches, pickles, light and dark cake, pink and white ice cream with cherries and apples."

Next day "us three 'spinsters'"—herself, Elizabeth, and Anna—walk half a mile to a neighbors' and stay for supper, then home "to visit with the boys again. Lots of fun." She cites further holiday activities—a movie at the Mystic, get-togethers in various relatives' homes: "Have a dandy fine time . . . Especially the wrestling match between Anna and Will."

At season's end, Bertha's cousins leave and Elizabeth returns to teaching. "Clean up the whole house after they are gone. Feel very punk." And no wonder, for she lives on the euphoria of parties and social activities, since her ordinary daily routine consists of housework. Fortunately, a neighbor six miles down the road invites Anna and Bertha for an oyster supper. "Home at about three." The scandalously late hour is proof to her scribe-self that she's still gadding about. Allowed to sleep until eleven, she offsets her sloth by doing fancywork and writing letters. The very next night, a young man's birthday party. "Have a fine time and splendid supper. Home at two."

After the holiday binge, the diary entries turn meager and sad. She doesn't bother to attend church on Sunday. "Arise at nine. Clean upstairs, dress, practice, read in Bible. Afternoon, read *At Cloudy Pass.* Evening at home and fool around." Once on her normal schedule, the writing consists of an almost impersonal recording: type of dress she's sewing, what the weather's like, the bedtime hour; it's typical of any nonliterary, unself-conscious diary. No attempts to examine what is happening or why; no inner dialogue. Mädchen Bertha, with her fair hair, strong cheekbones, pleasing Teutonic features, attractive clothes, and fun-loving manner, merely sets down the obvious. And yet the deeper motive for this diary writing is a yearning to come to terms with the passage of time in order to understand the meaning of her life, though this is never stated. I will have to fill in some of the gaps from the vantage point of decades later, long after her life achieved its shape.

Every child should be lucky enough to have an Aunt Bertha, available for fondling and hand-paddling, with an ample lap to climb up on. We did a lot of kissing and were foolish together, playing silly games. Her black seal coat in winter was great to stroke and awfully warm inside. Living in town with Grandma, running her store, she seemed happy enough. Sometimes among ourselves we might impudently speculate about Bertha's marrying, but we knew it was probably too late and had never heard of any interested suitor. She served as an adjunct parent, somebody always around, looking out for our interests—an ally, not a spy from the adult world. She had a lively mind, enjoyed reading, was musical. Why hadn't she become a teacher, like my mother and Bertha's sisters, Elizabeth and Mary?

BERTHA AT ABOUT THE TIME
THE DIARY WAS WRITTEN, 1913.

Was it a matter of character, family circumstance, or a combination
of both? Back then none of us thought to wonder much, which is
typical of the egotism of childhood; but now here is her diary, a
personal glimpse of her life fourteen years before I was born. I'm
surprised how immature she sounds for someone twenty-seven.

Mon. Jan. 13
    Remodel my mother's petticoat, my velvet dress, etc. Cold
day. Work on sheet in evening.

Tues. Jan. 14
      Sew a little in morning. P.M. work on point-lace curtain,
also in evening.

Wed. Jan. 15
      Wash in the morning. A big washing too. In the P.M. go to
town on a shopping trip. Make fancywork in eve. Iron.

Poor Bertha! It sounds dreary and she knows it. Things liven up
a bit when her first cousins, to whom she refers formally as the
"Misses Kruse," as if writing for the society page, arrive from Sioux
City for a visit. More parties, with the evening's success measured by
how late they stay up. Sunday morning she sleeps in, missing church,
but receives no scolding from "Pa" over such backsliding. Clearly my
notion of Grandfather as a fierce authoritarian when it came to
church going is all wrong. His daughters attend services only if they
feel like it, and throughout the diary Bertha tries a variety of
Protestant worship, even taking in a Catholic Mass, her attitude
suggesting social interest rather than religious conviction.

Tues. Jan. 21
      Finish two dresses for Ma and five aprons. In the evening
Hank & I go to the "fireman's dance." [My father is twenty-one
at this time.] Big crowd. Have a good time but do not dance.

Strange to think of her as a wallflower. Skilled at sewing and
adept at keeping house (though not an experienced cook—Anna
does that, along with "Ma"), wouldn't any man feel lucky having
Bertha for a wife? Her sleeping late might be thought a mark of
laziness, but her parents allow her to do it because she's still the
hopeful, marriageable daughter, princess of the household. She needs
proper rest in order to remain beautiful. For Anna, her thirty-year-
old sister, it's perilously close to being too late for matrimony.
      Bertha arises next day at ten and spends the morning "doing the
upstairs," which was probably in a state of polished cleanliness from
the going-over of the day before. She would be assigned this task
because the family's housekeeping standards were so high. Also, each
morning there were a number of beds to make—a woman's business;
the males didn't have to bother.

ANNA, C. 1910.

The same held true for my generation. I had a boy's outdoor chores list: gather eggs, feed and water the chickens, mow the lawn, weed the garden, drive the tractor in the grain harvest, tend blower in threshing. Mother or one of the two girls made all our beds each morning. To this day my wife complains that I had too many women picking up after me in early life—a pattern that began long before I was born.

Bertha's real occupation will gradually become more evident: not just Monday laundry, Tuesday ironing, Wednesday mending, but the business of sewing dresses and other garments, as well as needlework of all kinds. Bertha is solidly engaged in traditional

women's activities while awaiting matrimonial developments. As she
has been waiting a good many years. Her twenty-seventh birthday
approaches; she knows as well as everybody else how old that is in a
farm society. When will things change for her? How will the shift
occur? This is the promise the year 1913 holds: her big chance might
happen. She meets destiny halfway and will not miss a social
opportunity that might develop into suitable possibilities.

When courting matters arise, the diary becomes fuller, more
animated. For instance, with their neighbors holding a sale, she
knows it'll be a good chance to see people. Sixteen-year-old Jack
drives her over. "Have dinner, then go out to watch the sale a bit,
how things go."

Jan. 23
Cousins Rose & Clara, Julia Hemster, Kate, Emma & we have a
time. Say that we are to be sold too. John E. comes around and
invites us to a box social at O'Leary on Fri. eve. S.C. sport
around [an interested suitor from Sioux City]. Lots of fun. After
a bit, go in the house and help do the dishes. Go out and stay
there while horses are being sold. S. City sport leaves. Tells me
to get ready to go with him as he says he bought me. I'm ready,
I tell him. Later tell him I'll come down to S. City after a bit. He
sure was some sport. Stay awhile after it is over. Have lunch
before we go. John E. tells us again and again to be sure to
come to O'Leary. Want to go most very bad, but . . .

A transportation problem. The O'Leary dance hall (where
Lawrence Welk in later years would play engagements) was located
at a crossroads ten miles away. Finally she persuades Henry to drive
her and Anna to the box social. After baking two kinds of cake, they
hunt up containers in which to present them, gaily decorated.

Jan. 24
Have a program of reading by a Morningside College lady.
Very good. After that they sold the boxes. Get a Mr. Eyres for a
partner. He sure was some talker. Have a fine time during
supper. Joke on J.E.; he wants one of our boxes but doesn't get
any. After supper, talk with him and some other sports—then
sail for home. Lights give out on the way. Ha, sure treated us
fine out there, felt right at home.

Although both Anna and Bertha are invited to a neighbor's house the following night, their parents object: "Raise such howls that we stay at home. Made work at curtain in late P.M. & eve." Sunday, however, is for getting about. She watches a play in Remsen, *The Great Divide,* then visits with friends. "Edna tells more about the sport"—the Sioux City man met at the farm sale. It's reliable information, since her cousin Edna is from that metropolis. On Tuesday, "Card from Soo sport," making the world brighter.

Wed. Jan. 29
Beautiful day, just like spring. Patch, iron & press in morning.
In the P.M. make fancywork. Runaway team comes on yard.
Buggy overturned at gate. Pa catches and ties up the team. Pa &
Ma go down to gate & down the road. Soon we hear someone
call for help. Call boys & Pa & they get the car and go down.
Know by this time that it's Fred Meyen. Take him home . . .
broke two bones at the ankle. Oh, such excitement. Work on
curtain in eve.; started the third one today. Receive card from
sport at S.C.

Two cards in one week and her birthday in the offing. Things seem promising.

Sat. Feb. 1
My 27 birthday—do up the usual Sat. work. Had planned to go
to Soo City & have a good time on my birthday, but no, it had
to be too cold to be pleasant—

The moment, like so many others which might have provided a solution to the direction of her life, passes with nothing to show for it. But I wonder if she would have had the nerve to look up the Sioux City sport, had she gone.

Bertha's daily record of handiwork accomplishments attests to her worth and offsets the frivolity: she finishes sewing a curtain, attaches crocheted inserts to two pillowcases, and "stamps an eyelet centerpiece." She also begins preparations for her first trip out of state, to Hurley, South Dakota, where she will stay for several months with Elizabeth, who teaches in the high school.
After arriving and settling in with Elizabeth, she takes up

needlework during the hours she is alone while her sister is conducting classes. She begins by mending "a rip on Eliz's coat." Before long she is receiving sewing assignments from Hurley matrons, thereby justifying her extended stay. Meanwhile, a whole new territory of acquaintances opens up, among them perhaps a man who might become her husband.

By arriving in February with the snow blowing and wind howling, Bertha finds her life at first rather confining. She drops in at the school and watches Elizabeth coach the girls' basketball team and attends an evening game played against a rival town. On the first Saturday night, an oyster supper at the Methodist church, "Ralph Davis my partner." Days of entries follow that say mostly "Sew all day." A "blue-figured silk" for one lady, a white dress and a blue one for another, then a tan corduroy. There are a few entertainments: the Masonic quartet sings well, "but such a cold house that really could not enjoy it. Nearly froze when we got home—warmed up, & to roost. [Went to bed.]"

Despite the age gap, Bertha makes friends with Etta, one of Elizabeth's students. "Etta up to see us, and the following week, Eliz and I are invited out to supper at her home."

Under the attic eaves of the farmhouse, I discovered three letters from Etta to Elizabeth, with affectionate salutations: "My dear Sweetheart" and "My dear Beth." In one Etta says, "I don't know whether you love me or not anymore. I do so want to see you and talk with you. You always did me so much good. You are so far away that I can't make you hear. My love for you wasn't just a kid's affection. It was and is the real thing."

Apparently a schoolgirl's crush on the teacher—which Elizabeth probably tried to cool by distancing herself. Bertha on her Hurley visit seems unaware of these emotional undercurrents. She is quietly proud of Elizabeth for having been taken up by the leading families of the town: Etta's father is a prominent attorney; another friend's family owns the largest department store. These fathers take a proprietary interest in squiring Elizabeth and Bertha home after late nights out. Although Bertha is a paid seamstress for the smart ladies of Hurley, she suffers no loss of status—indeed, she feels equal to them all—for what she's doing to earn money is an acceptable occupation for a maiden awaiting possible matrimony.

Little develops that might be considered "courting." Instead, what takes place are amiable visits and excursions with Elizabeth and her girlfriends. Even a "kid party," in which the eight girls present "play and talk like kids." Bertha describes the "nice supper": "Table decorated with stick candy, mints & candles. First course: salad, pickles, rolls, and chocolate; second, peaches with whipped cream . . . fig newtons & the candy." They end the evening by eating the table decorations—just like kids.

The sewing goes on apace: "Worked on Mary's [her oldest sister, seldom mentioned here] new dress all day . . . Finished Mary's dress & started Daisy's striped voile." Finally, a glimmer of romance: at the end of March "John Webster calls" and takes Bertha and Elizabeth to a card party, where they play rummy and "Have a good time . . . John W. sees us home." Not exactly a date, since there were two of them on his hands, but a start—and he will persist for a while. With the arrival of April, better weather and an increase in social life: "Have an auto ride. Just a lovely day. Miss Abraham & Miss Carr call; home with Mr. Wray."

With her seamstress skills in great demand, her days are full. By the middle of the month she has turned out nine dresses and shirtwaist ensembles without a crimp in her pursuit of the local nightlife—the movies, a band concert, a cantata by the Choral Union, "The Resurrection Hope." In her spare time she's reading *The Rosary* ("Very good"), *Janet's College Career,* and *Homestead on the Hillside.*

There are evenings with girlfriends like Maude Mitchell, "over for a little while. Fun about our beaux. Ha." But will the final laugh be on Bertha if nothing much in Hurley changes her love life? "Etta and I get our seats for the class play. Etta brings me partway home. Bed at eleven." For days Bertha seems to live in an exclusively female world, with fittings, ice cream eating, and church doings, though she mentions attending a Mason's dance—again, with a girlfriend.

On April 23, "Mr. Eingrey comes in after me. Go out in the country for the first time since I left home." She is nostalgic for the land now that spring has come. Even in Hurley, with its modest population of a few thousand, a gulf exists between the town and the farm.

Sunday afternoon, May 4, while out walking with Elizabeth: "Are overtaken by Ruth & Etta & Stanley Browne. They invite us to go with them to Parker [a nearby town]. Of course we accept. Have a dandy ride. Go all over Parker & some parts a dozen times." The very next day, "Mr. C. & John come for me . . . Get a long auto ride in their new Reo." The possibilities of privacy that courting couples will discover in the automobile doesn't enter her head sufficiently to mention, perhaps because at the moment she is motoring with others.

The days pass quickly. "Finish up voile skirt" and "finish up waist," as well as a tan and pink girdle and a gray dress—a litany of accomplished work. But she also takes walks to pick violets, goes on car rides, and sits on the porch one evening "with Bee, Ada and John."

As the school term draws to a close, events connected with it predominate: "Attend the Junior reception in eve . . . Dress in my blue crepe de chine. Have nice time, serve fruit punch and wafers." Sunday, May 19: Baccalaureate services. Meanwhile, she's busy winding up the sewing projects. "Call at Welsh's to get my check. Call at Kellar's next to deliver a package. Then go to the movies. After the show see Mr. Browne." But again, Bertha is merely part of a crowd. "He treats Minnie Kellar, Minnie & Maude M., Eliz & I to ice cream. Walk home with Maude." The next day, commencement, followed by a forlorn stroll with Maude, "Go down & up 'Lovers Lane.'"

Elizabeth returns home to Remsen for the long summer vacation, and now Bertha sleeps alone, having doubled up with her sister all these months. After a week's side trip to Bridgewater, South Dakota, where she has been engaged to do some sewing, she arrives at the Remsen depot, met by her brother Henry. He reports on the upcoming social calendar. No time for rest. "Get home, undress & pack box for social. Mine's a suitcase covered with nile crepe & silk lavender ribbons. Go to social & have a good time." Next day, Sunday, another event of the same sort: "Wash dishes & repack our boxes & off for the social again. Have a nice time . . . Earl Miller my partner. Home at twelve."

Finally she has to settle down. The novelty of having been away is over; now it's washing, ironing, cleaning the back stairs, lawn work, and helping out at a neighbor's in feeding the corn shellers.

"In the evening the 'spinsters' and Henry went out for an auto ride," and one Sunday "the 'Big Three' [as she mockingly calls herself, Elizabeth, and Anna] go on a 'man hunt,' but like always, don't hear or see one." The holiday is spoiled in any case because she has her period; "feel punk all day."

From most of her diary entries it's hard to remember she lives on a farm, though in later years when I knew her, she was an ardent gardener and loved digging in the dirt. Now she views herself as much too refined for any of that. But on July 1, after ironing in the morning and molding rose-colored beads in the afternoon, her brothers enlist her help: she is to lead "the horse, 'Jack,' for the hay fork." When a shout from the men in the barn indicated that the fork in the hay rack had been securely set, Bertha would "gee-up" the horse and pull on its bridle, making the rope taut and lifting the forkload to the rafters, where it hit a traverse and was shunted along to the intended mow. The men would trip the fork, the hay would drop, and Bertha would walk the horse back to the barn. Not a lady's sort of work, but an honest assignment and a relief from housework.

Wed. July 2
Decide to go to Garner per auto for the "4th" [to visit their Greiman cousins]. Such a time to get ready. Fix up my sash, etc., in the morning; in the noon hour go to town and shop some necessary articles. In the P.M. fix up some of my "duds" and pack . . . looks like rain now all is ready for the much talked of trip, but still live very much in doubt as to whether we really will get started.

A family snapshot of Henry at the wheel of a horseless carriage, covered on top but open at the sides, shows it to be a vehicle not suitable for rainy weather.

Thurs. July 3
Arise a little before five after a restless night. Resume packing clothes, lunch, etc. At fifteen of six we start for our trip. Dandy riding. Stop a little while south of Paulina, a little while at Spencer, have dinner under the trees near Emmetsburg. Stop for an hour and continue until Algona; here get out and go to Drug store and get something to drink . . . Stop at a schoolhouse and at 6:15 land at Katters'.

Their mother's people make much of this surprise visit. Although Bertha has a headache on the Fourth, she records, "Dress

& get ready to spend the day at Clear Lake." Soon they are joined by other Greiman cousins, listen to patriotic speeches, sit in the park chatting, eat a picnic lunch, and as if they are children again, enjoy merry-go-round rides, then "pop, lemonade, and ice cream." They walk down to where they bathe, "and although it's hot, do not go in." At five o'clock a group of them take the launch *Princess* to Oakwood and Bayside. "Beautiful over there. Lay on grass etc. Go back on *Victoria*." Following a restaurant supper, "Look at fireworks for a short time and as it looks a good bit like rain, pull for home. Get there at ten, a few minutes later a shower . . . Have lunch and then for bed. Good day. That's the way 'the glorious Fourth of 1913' was spent; 50th anniversary of Gettysburg."

Next day they call on Uncle Will Greiman, then motor to Uncle Fred's, where they will spend the night. Bertha reports, all "dumbfounded to see us. Very glad." Nobody seems to use the telephone; all social engagements are done in person. Bertha relishes the outpouring of family hospitality. Although my childhood in the thirties was blessed with a many-layered clan life, it was nothing compared to the family shorings of the generation before. The luck of birth placed one in an ever-extending connection of kinship; so many folks, and all of them *ours.*

The visitors attend church and "take a front seat," acceding to the drama their presence lends. The rest of the day is devoted to eating, talking, and more excursions on Clear Lake, ending with evening services at the Methodists'. "After church, bum. Joe S. treats us all to ice cream and soda. Have bushels of fun in the restaurant. Ha. Art a crackerjack. Ha." Was he?—this cousin of my father's, whose middle name I carry. Knowing so little of my father, I cling to small clues as to what he and his friends were like. "Fool around in Katters' yard until 11:30. Bed." They play some sort of joke on Anna. She usually gave as good as she got. In these off-moments when nothing much seems to be happening, I listen to time pass for them, feel their lives in the daily living.

On the trip home, "no trouble or anything," and each of the towns they pass through is mentioned, as if Bertha is trying to fix herself upon the map of Iowa. Arriving at the farm, "Pack away all our things. Soak the washing. Now for work." She can only feel right about their extravagantly good time by balancing it with hard labor. She knows the purpose of life isn't merely the pursuit of happiness but moral improvement as well. The way to that is not through pleasure.

Bertha continues to note daily activities but with scant elaboration and dodges the chief question: How much more "promise" of a future can she take? When will she and her family have to acknowledge that marriage isn't likely? Should she remain passively at home, as Anna is doing? All over the country, single women of all ages were keeping house for "the folks," enjoying financial protection; and when the parents died, they usually inherited enough to see themselves out and into eternity.

I doubt if Bertha frankly discussed marital prospects with her mother, but among her sisters it seems to have been a constant subject. The web of cousins and close girlfriends both sustains and suffocates; it sets her in a respectable circle but makes it difficult for possible suitors to get through to her personally. In Bertha's world there was no agreed-upon route to marriage. With no savvy marriage broker to make a match, some perfectly eligible daughters could easily be left out. Parents reticent with their daughters regarding such matters or laissez-faire in attitude might discover too late that destiny often needs a helping hand. John and Louisa Harnack, with four girls on the marital scene, appear to have merely sat back, waiting for whatever might come about.

When the Chautauqua erects a tent in town, Bertha has an admirable, cultural destination for three nights in a row, though one evening "stay about 20 minutes or so when it begins to rain . . . go home. Mad." After one Chautauqua program, she writes, "Watch them dance for a while. Home & to bed." She's a viewer of the fun but not a participant.

Thurs. Aug. 7
Cut and peeled apples from 8 until 12. Felt like an apple myself. After dinner packed the eggs, watered the chickens, etc. Read— *The House of the Whispering Pines.*

Sunday could be gloomy if the leisure one deserved and expected was not forthcoming. "Slept late, up and lay around, practiced my music; sore bunion, can hardly walk. Read, sleep, and practice in P.M. Sit by the roadgate awhile in eve. and eat apples." Poor Bertha!

She feels so depressed that by the time a house-to-house agent shows up on Tuesday with his wares and joshing line of gab, she and Anna, though busy with clothes washing, pause and "have a dickens of a time." Anything for diversion, even the slick Watkins man trying to be charming because he hopes to make a sale.

Pickling crab apples, canning two baskets of plums and store-bought pears—doing up eight quarts in all—give a sense of accomplishment; however, "Misery, but it is hot!" Kettles and tubs steaming away on the stoves make the kitchen hellish.

One Sunday, "In the eve. the three 'spinsters' go for a 'manhunt'—See Theodore and Mike Jen. and later the Kramer girls on their way out, so of course turn back." Wouldn't want others to think they were desperate; too much forwardness would also certainly spoil romantic prospects.

At last, a real diversion! "When we are in bed, Johnny tells us that Pa and Hank are going to Sheldon Fair tomorrow."

Fri. Aug. 23
Get there at 9:30. Seems so queer to be at a county fair.
Everything so small . . . After dinner watch the races, ride on
merry-go-round, etc. Also see an airship make two very
successful flights; motorcycle race. Premium parade. See the
prize babies get their pictures taken, etc.
    Also had my fortune told, something like this it ran:
"Good girl," lots of friends, but many of them false. As a
teacher I would meet with great success. My talents were not
cultivated. Great talent for music and art, especially music. By
music I could make the most money. At the end of this year a
position of trust was going to be offered me which I would
hesitate to accept, but which I should by all means do, as I was
capable of filling it. In religion I was earnest & sincere and
wouldn't change my view for anyone. Would have two suitors.
One dark & one medium dark. Should & would take the
medium dark. Would be happy, but a lady who had caused
trouble now already would [bring] still more right along. But by
tact everything would become all right & she would cease to
bother. Man jealous and quick-tempered, so would have spats
"now and then," but he would be a devoted companion. Marry
twice. First time for love, 2nd for riches. 2nd man an elderly
man whom I could have married when I married young man.

Have already met them both. Am popular but could be more so
if friends were not so jealous. Jealous people succeeded in
robbing me of much pleasure. Liked everything refined and
elegant and loathed the reverse.

Bertha seems to half believe this nonsense, perhaps because here at
last someone is focusing on the central matter. From her hours of
sitting by the roadside, looking off across the field, to this fortune-
teller in a tent, Bertha seeks encouraging news.

Any stranger could see that she liked "everything refined"—
which might give a farmer-suitor pause, since country life was often
coarse. But her elegance and interest in music and art would appeal
to a man who recognized that farm life often needed lightening.
However, most rural housewives succumbed quickly—too many
babies and not enough help—and the finer things were set aside and
eventually forgotten. Some men perhaps found Bertha a bit silly,
dreamy, and sentimental, although she cultivated this aura, echoing
the popular songs and fiction of the day, in order to appear alluringly
feminine.

In early September she writes: "Pack all my duds & do other
little things," for tomorrow she leaves with Elizabeth for Sioux City,
where both will attend a business college. "Hurrah. At last I am
going to school. The dearest ambition of my life."

If true, she could have gone years ago; now she convinces herself
it's just the ticket. Some direction must be set; she cannot simply
continue with her life as it is.

Beyond high school, Bertha had taken only a few university
short courses, none resulting in a certificate qualifying her for a
career. She had memorized most of the famous poems of Whittier,
Longfellow, and Bryant, which she often recited for her nieces and
nephews in later years as we sat together on the porch swing. Like a
teacher, she monitored our progress and encouraged us to show off
our talents, especially in music. Some summer evenings Bertha and
Elizabeth would arrive in time for supper, carrying with them a
covered dish by way of contribution. Before we ate we would gather
in the parlor; Ruth or Ken might play the piano or Lois her flute, me
the clarinet. One night as Ken was in the middle of a delicate, moving
Chopin étude, Bertha suddenly erupted: "Oh dear! We forgot the

jello!" After that we weren't so sure of the depth of Bertha's appreciation of music.

In Sioux City she attends arithmetic and typing classes in the morning; in the afternoon there's home study and housekeeping. After a few weeks she's back on the farm for a brief visit. "Have the thrashers. Big supper, eat too much. Bad spell of cramps that night." She tries to hold close a city part of herself: "Look at fashions while thrashers ate," paying them no attention at all. "Then get the washing things ready. Get the kettle on, wash dishes, hunt my winter clothes . . . after that help with dinner . . . Feel miserable all day. Glad when night comes. Talk late that night."

Upon her return to Sioux City, the entries are simple, often just "School all day" or recording personal errands that take her to various shops. On one occasion Elizabeth and Bertha inspect a greenhouse. "Sport showed us thru. Such pretty mums." She never misses a chance to note a lively gent in close proximity—perhaps because there are few of them.

Near the end of the diary I understand this record better. The doings of her family are public matters and completely known; only what concerns *her* will be admitted here, a corner of privacy.

Still, questions remain. What brought about Bertha's decision to undertake business training? The idea might have popped up when Elizabeth took a leave in order to acquire teaching skills in commercial subjects. Bertha may have teamed up with her in the Sioux City adventure for the heck of it, with no clear career objectives in mind. Anyone could see how restless and anxious she was.

Now in the city, in the dialogue with her private self she can no longer maintain a stance of promise—or at least not in the same adolescent way, for her business courses would lead to some kind of job. Her means of livelihood for the coming years was about to be established. Since it no longer felt right to her to simply "be" at home, she would make her way in the larger world of the city. Elizabeth was out and away, enjoying her own life. Bertha would do the same.

After a number of routine diary entries, she stops the effort in mid-November, finally aware perhaps that the repetitive aspect of her days insistently points up her changed circumstances. She resumes the chronicle the following March, when she travels alone to Jacksonville, Florida, to soak up the spring sunshine as she

BERTHA IN HER GARDEN AT REMSEN, C. 1940.

recuperates from an illness. While viewing the passing landscape from the train window and encountering new experiences, she tries to become a writer in order to do the trip justice. She places herself in her own history by means of geography and begins finally, at age twenty-eight, to sound like a mature woman.

Travel always quickened Bertha's spirits. She liked to measure her life against others, compare places, seek out the unusual. She once laughingly remarked to us children that if she owned a string of tourist cabins in Minnesota and another set in the South, she could enjoy agreeable climates at appropriate times of the year—and best of all, she would be in continual contact with travelers, from whom one could always learn much. But such a vagabond destiny would not be hers.

No doubt Bertha would remind me that few people are aware of crucial life decisions the moment they are made. I shouldn't try to pin down the exact moment her affairs took one direction rather than another. Nor was there a specific moment of realization that no marriage offers would likely come her way—or at least no proposal that could be seriously entertained. Which didn't mean she'd abandoned hope of it happening. *That* would be underestimating her faith in the unexpected.

Disappointed by life? Not in the least—or not much of the time. I can't presume to know when dashed hopes left off and practical adjustment to her situation began. She clerked in stores and had some business experience before she and a Danish-born partner set up a hat and dress shop in Remsen upon her parents' retirement to town in 1920. But settling down to a career didn't necessarily mean her life couldn't change suddenly in other ways—who might know when? Perhaps on a buying trip to Omaha or Kansas City, when some "sport" in the rag trade handed her an amusing line, and she took him up on it.

Whether or not in hopes of such a possibility, Bertha kept herself attractive, dressed in a genteel style. Discreetly penciled eyebrows, makeup that covered wrinkles, little lipstick or rouge. Even in middle age her hair was so adroitly colored a mousy, soft, blondish-brown that it was difficult to believe it had been treated. One never glimpsed undyed roots or any gray strands.

In her nieces and nephews she would enjoy a substitute progeny—like having children without the attendant discord and mess; a more orderly relationship. Grandma and Bertha's house became our town home, where we could go after school while waiting to be fetched or after church-pageant practice. Bertha, with or without Grandma, was our regular Sunday dinner guest—or we were at her table, which we much preferred. In our Sunday best and having bathed the night before, we were respectable "company." She would set out her best linen napery; the Haviland china and pinging crystal; the lustrous, Grecian-patterned Towle silverware.

The art nouveau and art deco furnishings of the house—from the purple and gray Chinese rug in the dining room to the silver-etched dinnerware which had been fired in the farm kiln years before—were lessons to us in modern taste. We noted the imitation French provincial buff-colored furniture in Grandma's bedroom. The Hollywood-inspired twin beds in the upstairs guest room were

AUNTS BERTHA, ELIZABETH, AND ANNE,
WITH THE FARMHOUSE IN THE
BACKGROUND, MID-1940s.

covered with elaborately worked spreads, embroidered throws, ruffly pillows, and on the dresser, lace-edged scarves and hair-receivers. So much feminine refinement here, representing hours of painstaking work, and the original purpose of it all had been to accumulate a trousseau. Precisely because there was no husband for Bertha, or snot-nosed kids, these pretty things had never been ignored or forgotten. Instead, her years unfolded in a richly detailed setting. Girlish promises remained forever in the offing. Finally her treasures were laid up for me and others of my generation to haul away—if we cared to. Eventually much of the booty was given to anybody who spoke up, or it was sold when the house was emptied.

Bertha did not live long enough to have to worry about the final disposition of her handiwork, the efforts of a lifetime. Anne and

Elizabeth did that later, after Bertha's death. They insisted that my wife take one of the twelve-place settings of hand-decorated china; the punch bowl painted with cherries, plus the goblets that went with them; the gold-banded grape juice pitcher and cups; quilts in log cabin, morning glory, and tulip designs; punchwork tablecloths embossed with the initial "H"; heavy damask napkins—all our suitcases could hold. They knew the time had come.

In the late 1940s when Bertha fell ill, the rest of us were told little, cancer being such a taboo, and since it was ovarian cancer, even more unmentionable. The first operation she underwent did not cure her. Bertha lived alone now, following Grandma's death, so Anne left Worthington, Minnesota, to return home to help. In summer, with school over, Elizabeth arrived to bolster Bertha's resolve to fight the disease.

The three sisters had always preferred nontraditional medical treatments when possible and believed ardently in the wisdom of folk remedies. They thought their chiropractor did more good than any physician they'd been to. Hardly surprising, therefore, that in desperation they hit upon Joanna Brandt's Grape Cure, which all of them undertook in order to help Bertha maintain a diet consisting solely of grapes—skins, seeds, and all. At first a few grapes, preferably fresh ones (not raisins or bottled grape juice) of varying acidity and sweetness, were to be eaten every few hours, seven meals a day for a period of perhaps months. "A loathing for grapes may indicate the presence of much poison in the system and the need of another short fast," wrote Joanna Brandt in her book, *The Grape Cure*, which I found on the farm among Uncle Jack's piles of family memorabilia. "We hear of over-zealous relatives forcing grapes down the throats of unfortunate patients. This is a mistake."

Well I should think!

"Loss of strength is due to the presence of poisons in the system," she emphasizes. "The patient continues to weaken under the grape diet and under the complete fast, until the poison has been expelled."

It didn't work out that way. Bertha weakened all right, and the cancerous cells proliferated. One night Aunt Anne—who had spent much of her life in the farmhouse kitchen and during her salaried years while married to Ernest, as a cook in a railway restaurant in Worthington, Minnesota—sneaked down to the basement and fried a porkchop for herself on the kerosene stove which Grandma had used in summer when it was too hot upstairs. The pungent smell of the meat permeated the house. Elizabeth scolded Anne for this breach of faith, but Bertha intervened, begging them to call off the diet; she'd had enough. However, Elizabeth felt they hadn't given the Grape Cure a chance to do its work. She may have quoted the text they were living by: "It is safe to say that the first seven to ten days on grapes only would be required to clear the stomach and bowels of their ancient accumulations. And it is during this period that distressing symptoms often appear . . . The purification of every part of the body must be complete before new tissue can be built." But even Elizabeth's strong faith in this last-resort treatment could not obscure the fact that Bertha was dying.

I was two hundred miles from home then, hitting the books hard at Grinnell College, hoping to make a grade-point average respectable enough to win a scholarship to graduate school. I had my eye on the Lydia Roberts Fellowship at Columbia, since competition was restricted to Iowa-born graduates of Iowa colleges.

The call came: Bertha's funeral was to be on the day of the Graduate Record Examination. Columbia required that I take the test and no special case could be made for me. I felt torn, knowing that my explanation over the phone to the folks at home did not quite excuse my callous behavior. I heard in my voice a lack of caring, a shirking of duty to the memory of someone who'd been an intimate part of my early days.

Yes, of course they understood why I couldn't come. I must certainly do what was best, in order to advance. I wasn't to feel bad; it couldn't be helped.

And so I was absent from the cortege behind Bertha's casket. Part of my past seemed ending—and had for some time. I won the fellowship to Columbia and in a few months would be off to New York. My refusal to jeopardize my future over a matter of sentiment and family duty foretold the pattern my life was taking, with all steps leading relentlessly away.

NATIVE OF THE WILD WEST

Our family's leavings in the attic, which may have looked like ordinary household junk, still held resonances for me, and our efforts to dislodge it seemed a desecration. Lois's husband, Rex, being an outsider, was best equipped for the task at hand, though he respected what she and I were going through. Indeed, he had done much the same in his mother's house only a few months previously. Now he backed the pickup close, below the open eastern attic window. Through this porthole we heaved brown-paper garment containers with cracked glassine panels after only a glance inside at the moth-eaten coats, bathrobes, and blanket-lined jackets. No market in these parts for worn clothing of this vintage, I am told, but I save some period dresses and silk slips from the thirties and forties for my suitcase. Family presents. Or to be used for barter with the proprietor of Grandma's Attic in Saratoga Springs.

As I gather the clothes in my arms, clouds of dust arising, a revulsion sets in: I'm eager to have done with this. Out the window any old way, these discards flutter haphazardly to the frozen ground. Books for burning—outdated college texts, yearbooks, scrap albums for school projects—make easy missiles; I sometimes hit the truck box below and save Rex the trouble of having to collect them from the yard. Later Rex will load all the detritus and haul it to his farm's trash-burning spot. No place here to start a bonfire safely, the buildings being too close, the fields rented out. In any case, one would want to stay near the fire for hours to keep an eye on it. Some of the more flammable stuff would burn like dry faggots, but a lot of it would smolder a long time.

From recreational junkshop-touring in and around Saratoga Springs, I knew the current value of most of these artifacts of middle-class American life, now so pop culture and collectible. Alas, Lois's authentic Shirley Temple doll was a mangled mess; my Mickey

Mouse watch couldn't be found—had the thieves taken it? Sister Ruth's toy piano still tinkled hopelessly out of tune. Lois's doll dishes set, missing a number of pieces, looked respectable, though the miniature cardboard house itself had suffered under too many layers of dust. The movie projector didn't seem to have all its parts, and the comedy filmstrips had probably been disposed of as a fire hazard. My archery equipment, very little worn, might fetch something, but who knew how much? The wood-burning stylus, an Aunt Elizabeth Christmas present to all of us but seldom used, would probably blow a fuse, so we didn't try to find out if it still worked.

I kept calling a halt. "No, not the laundry mailing box; maybe I can use it somehow." Brown canvas covered a sturdy cardboard, reinforced frame; two straps and buckles and a reversible address label with "Mrs. John Harnack, Remsen, Iowa" on one side and one of our names with a college address on the other.

Or "Lois, wouldn't you like that ironstone plate? Look, it's hallmarked." But she, having accumulated quite a stash already, wasn't to be persuaded and said instead: "Why don't *you* take it?"

By now a second-floor room was filling up with items we hadn't been able to send to oblivion. Perhaps we were bogging down and losing our resolve to get this job over. Rex was dubious about the monetary value of some of these artifacts which I said should be sold if we ourselves didn't want them. He knew how little the secondhand dealer had given for the downstairs furniture.

In Le Mars I located a shop willing to take consignments. But they didn't know what to do with my copy of the *Chicago Tribune,* headlined "DEWEY WINS," which I'd bought the morning after the 1948 presidential election in a Grinnell news shop. I ended up presenting it to a high school acquaintance who dealt in old books and magazines. Aunt Anne's quilts and Bertha's fancywork of all kinds, when in good condition, I packed away for personal use—and well they have served us ever since. These family items, still touching my daily life, have a nurturing effect. But I sometimes wonder if the downside is a mysterious, collaborative holding-back, leading me to refuse the evidence of time passing. I recognize Mother's patch at the knee of an old pair of my Levi's and touch the stitches as if they were sutures. What is the meaning of this elegant patch? Is it holding my life together? Part of the tyranny of objects or a seductive comfort—which?

In the consignment shop, once I view our attic goods labeled with dollar signs and placed among the flotsam as prized "virgin" stock (regular checkers, I'm told, keep a close eye out for such things), I realize that in this setting our family's connection to the stuff will soon melt away. I have seen similar merchandise in other ragtag shops, still physically hanging around in the consumer world but divested of their auras. The saddest of all are picture collections on sale not so much for the unidentifiable photographs mounted between handsome board covers but for the decorated album itself, the frame superseding the thing framed.

No wonder I soon felt that mass cremation was a suitable solution for most of the attic remains. At the end of each day Rex would haul his truckload to the pasture just below their farmhouse and set fire to the heap. Some evenings, long after dark, the bonfire coals glowed beyond Lois's winter-covered garden, now and then flaring up as a breeze fanned a reluctant bit into combustion. If I awoke in the small hours of early morning and looked out into the dark, I would see the carbuncle, red and alive. This was how we kept the home fires burning now.

In the light of day the ashy remains with metal oddments and pieces of unburnable materials made a small mound. When our attic job was all done, Rex expected to scoop the pile up with his manure buck and dispose of it in his junk heap; the junk pile itself would eventually be buried in order for the decay of the ages to work. The trouble with farming is that everything must be carried to the very limits and even beyond. No prettying up of existence; no avoiding the tasks attendant upon the mere business of living and dying. Nor any room for illusion.

I would follow behind Rex's truck each night in my rented car, the backseat crammed with saved goods to be sold, kept, or deliberated over. Rex drove fast but I tried to keep up, my eyes ahead of the light beams and fixed upon the doomed load he carried those forty miles on blacktop roads. We seldom encountered another car, as if we were engaged in secret, illegal work. Should the debris be piled too high, occasionally some of it blew off. I'd stop the car to snatch back whatever had been trying to get away, scrambling into the ditch along fencerows, wondering what stray piece of our lives I would find that needed to be reclaimed from the public domain—if only to be disposed of properly at last. Sometimes at this late stage

I felt unable to let go of an item we'd designated trash. Maybe it hadn't been given a fair shake; perhaps we'd been too hasty in our decision. For proper evaluation of everything no doubt months would be needed, not these few reckless days of tidying up a century of family life. But none of us had time for it—or the stomach.

Maybe I recognized a blue enamel pan I thought I wanted or a wooden crate with a colorful antique label. I would grab these things off the load "to think about it." Occasionally—rather eerily—objects in need of salvage presented themselves to my attention. One evening a curved, wooden-back shoebrush cascaded off the truck ahead and almost hit my windshield. I didn't know what the missile was until I finally found it in the ditch turf, its black letters reading "Le Mars Marble Works"—an advertising memento from the tombstone dealer. Merchants used to give out all sorts of knickknacks as part of their promotion, not just the ubiquitous calendars at year's end. I raked the brush across my knee: strong black bristles. In the years since, whenever I clutch it for use, I read the legend and ponder the

ELIZABETH, C. 1910.

possible connection between cemetery headstones and shoes in need of buffing. I haven't figured it out as yet.

Tired as we were after a day's work, Lois and I could not resist perusing some of the findings brought back to her warm house, as if this too was appropriate and part of the ritual. A time for last things. A kind of wake for the whole family.

What do we know about them, these people we lived with, whose lives intertwined with ours when we were growing up? They formed our attitudes and character; variations on the theme of oneself. We have a right to know who they really were, for truths of that kind provide a way into the mysteries of one's own personality, which never can be fully self-explored.

When I began reading Aunt Elizabeth's diary of her freshman year (1907–08) at the Normal School near Cedar Falls, I hoped to find her distinct voice somewhere in the pages. I could imagine her making the decision to become a teacher, persuading her parents to let her ride the Illinois Central train eastward, the college being not far from where her Greiman uncles, aunts, and cousins lived. Many from Remsen had gone or were going, for what other career might a girl pursue? The value of education for advancement in life was a well-known fact. Teachers enjoyed exceptionally high respect, though they endured some of the lowest salaries. Furthermore, her sister Mary was already a teacher and doing nicely.

I dip into the diary:

Thurs. Sept. 5
Went to school. Rescheduled. Studied in the evening.
Went down town after drawing material.

And so on—days of it. In the paucity of detail I catch the unformed, inarticulate girl Elizabeth was then, who resists to some extent the idea of doing a diary. Perhaps the notations might serve as memory jogs. If in later years she ever cares to recall just what happened to her in the tall, gaunt structure on Normal Hill, she will only have to open these pages and all will come back. But I doubt she ever did. This small exercise book was left under the attic eaves, forgotten—until this day when the leavings of all our lives are being turned over a final time.

If Elizabeth *had* bothered to glance at the pages written in clear, proper penmanship, she would have found her remarks as cryptic and incomplete or merely boringly routine as I do now. The act of recording implies significance of some sort, but here I see mostly brief stabs at noting activities merely because they happened.

Yet, there's no denying that this is an important phase of Elizabeth's life. She has embarked upon the first stage of her adventure in the outer world: the challenge of equipping herself

CAROLINE LANG, MY MOTHER,
AS SHE LOOKED C. 1910.

properly for a successful career. Now she interacts with more people who are not relatives than she has ever dealt with before. Will they find her attractive? Wish to become friends? Will her teachers note that she's somebody special? All signs must be promising, for it is her conviction that the world lies before her to be conquered, and now is clearly the time to begin. Upon graduation, under her yearbook photograph, she will be characterized as follows: "Native of the wild west. Basketball star. Member of the Yankee Band. Excels her opponents in hockey. Consumer of frappé. America's most famous lecturer on 'Our Duty.' 'A pusher, not a knocker.'" Normal School at Cedar Falls was Elizabeth's first significant triumph, and she went on from there.

Elizabeth quickly exhibits enough gumption to seek out the courses she wants: "Changed schedule for the fifth time." She signs up for a drawing class, rents a piano, and begins practicing in earnest. Soon she organizes excursions to Cedar Falls and Waterloo, appears at receptions, attends concerts; always there, ready for anything going. She's an admired presence among the dormitory girls. Carrie, my mother-to-be, is mentioned as one of her friends, as well as Mabel, Carrie's stepsister. Carrie at seventeen, a dark-haired, sloe-eyed beauty, cannot believe in her attractiveness. In any case those who are natural leaders, like Elizabeth, hold the focus of attention.

One senses a life in which the students and teachers mingle at all hours, almost like one big family. "Worked trig problems in Prof Wright's room. Cornelia & I went to see Miss Madsen a little while."

And there are parties:

Fri. Sept. 27
Rained all day. School. Studied in library until after 4. Postal from Mary K. The red-headed kid talked with me in library. Studied. Francis & Kate—in our room dressed as a man & Kate as a 16 year old. Grace invited us down. The whole house down. F. & K. in costume. Told stories, made fudge. Sang German songs. To bed after eleven.

The following day, having been invited to join the Ossoli sorority, she undergoes initiation.

Sat. Sept. 28
Dressed up & had picture taken (A & I). Anna & I went to
society. Initiated—Conducted by marshall to pledge.
Questioned. Name—Age. How many lovers, names, etc.
Cakewalk. Roll ball with the nose. Embrace statue. Give rhyme
with Ossoli, etc. Home after ten.

I note the satisfaction in winning over her peers; and the teachers
also, gratifyingly, appreciate her intelligence and talents. "Miss
Graham said I had a fine hand to play," Elizabeth reports, and the
teacher urges that she "specialize in music" but though flattered,
Elizabeth keeps her options open and records "First work in
gymnasium." She will excel in basketball and later coach the girls'
team in Hurley, South Dakota, and elsewhere.

Sat. Oct. 5
Cleaned room before breakfast. After breakfast patched clothes
& fixed skirts. Anna & I up big town [to Cedar Falls] after
dinner [in the afternoon]. Walked down & back. Got back & got
ready to go to woods. Frances, Lula, Theresa, Carrie, Anna & I.
Took the 4 o'clock car. Had a fine time gathering nuts. When
the baskets were filled we had supper near the river. Had bread,
pickles & dried beef. Admired the beautiful scenery along the
Cedar River. Heard the car coming & ran as fast as we could.
Got it in time & got a seat too. Got to Cedar Falls & had to wait
a long time. Finally the car came. Jumped the track at first turn.
All had to get off. Theresa fell off, nuts spilled. Got on again &
got to Normal Hill tired but happy. Stood on the back end of
car. Had a circus. Nell & I wrote a character sketch after
supper. To bed at 11.

School-girl stuff; a whole year of it. Thinking of the mature woman
I knew, her diary reveals only a characteristic push to get ahead. In
clearing out the attic I found a bundle of letters *I* had written home
from Grinnell my first year. The tenor is much the same.

Documents more difficult to assess are those letters from Etta,
a high school student from Hurley, South Dakota. The letters were
written to Elizabeth during the year she and Bertha attended business
college in Sioux City (1913–14) and several years after. Through the
mails, Elizabeth has been helping Etta on her speeches and written

assignments. Etta calls her "Dear Sweetheart" and says "Your ideas were fine and will certainly help a lot." In a cheeky, familiar tone, she reports on local news: who's sick, how the teams are doing, who got married. "Elizabeth, can't you find a fellow in that great big city? I am rather worried about *the* man. Are you real sure he doesn't belong to you? I hope not because it would make me jealous." Then she signs off: "Well sweetheart, I guess this is all . . . I don't see why you can't come and see me. You know the door is always open and you will be always welcome . . . With lots of love, Etta."

Another communication from Etta, April 20, 1914, begins this way:

> My dear Sweetheart,
>   You can't imagine how glad I was to get your letter. I was worried to death for fear you were angry at something I wrote in my last letter . . . For two whole weeks (it seems a month) I went down to the post office . . . Elizabeth, I want you to come and see me. If I could reach you I would shake you good. Drop that confounded (excuse me) work and come . . . [If] you just stay down there much longer and don't come up, I am coming down with the strongest magnet I can get and attract you. We are studying about them now. Which are you, a South or North pole?

In those days, would any schoolgirl write to her twenty-five-year-old teacher in this manner? No one can know the exact nature of this relationship, but most teachers—me included—have had acolytes move in close, unmindful of boundaries, insisting that no distance should exist between sympathetic people of similar age. Even the most on-guard teacher has difficulty at times fending off the attentions of a determined pupil. I can imagine Elizabeth's somewhat lonely lot in Hurley, with perhaps no companionable teacher on the staff. Etta's schoolgirl crush may have been a welcome diversion.

In another letter Etta says, "I am so glad you are back in South Dakota. I didn't like to have you in Utah." Elizabeth had spent a term in Salt Lake City, greatly intrigued by the Mormon civilization and particularly struck by their neatness. She told us years later of spring cleaning in Utah, which included washing down the outside walls of houses. But now she is teaching in Fort Pierre, on the edge

ELIZABETH (in the center) WITH HER BASKETBALL TEAM,
HURLEY, SOUTH DAKOTA, 1913.

of the Badlands, where the Middle West ends and the true West begins. She was thrown on her own resources and in subsequent years would recount tales of bullies who tried to make mischief in her school and how she had bested them in that rough, half-pioneer town. A woman alone had to know how to take care of herself.

Sept. 12, 1915

My dear Beth:

I hope you will forgive me dear for not answering your lovely letter before. I haven't any excuse to offer, just laziness I guess . . . Got the notion in my head that some one had written and told you some things and you were disgusted with me; didn't know whether to write or not. So you can imagine how relieved I was to get your letter . . . I am going to write my sister Mae and let her know where you are. Hope you will look each other up.

[Smudge mark]
This is a kiss

Etta messed the bottom of the page, then tried to make a valentine of it.

She continues: "I suppose you would like to hear some Hurley news." One boy has "a terrible case on a girl by the name of Peterson," another couple got married, one former classmate is clerking in a store, another teaches country school.

> Saw Florence Judd when she was here. She smiled at me real
> sweetly. I don't know whether her baby is a boy or girl. I
> suppose you will stop and see her on your way home. Ahem!
> Wouldn't be in her boots for anything. I used to worry my head
> off for fear it was you who was going with him instead of her.
> Was much relieved when I found out differently.

If Florence has stolen Elizabeth's boyfriend, Etta imagines the frosty scene should Elizabeth confront her. Etta, placing herself as a rival for Elizabeth's affections, is happy to dismiss this romantic adventure, relieved that her "sweetheart" is still a free agent.

> Ah Beth, this letter seems so cold . . . I know I have done wrong
> but I am trying so hard to cover it up and forget.

Overstepping the line, emotionally? Would that be the "wrong"?

> Please help me, Beth. I need your help more now than ever. If
> you feel towards me like you always did. If you do not love me,
> pray for an enemy . . .

These letters provide only a fragment of a story, with no resolution. Did Etta eventually marry, or did she find other idols to "fall for"? In any case, the lively, attractive girls' basketball coach of Hurley High moved farther and farther away. Affections could spill over in many directions in those innocent, pre-Freudian times, and no one thought it peculiar. Yet for girls the standard was known and fixed: you fell in love with a man, married, bore children. Otherwise, you became an old maid, a status to be avoided if at all possible. The hard, round kernels at the bottom of the popcorn bag were called "old maids," failures at opening up.

ELIZABETH AND BERTHA
AS PORTRAYED BY A HOLLYWOOD PHOTOGRAPHER, 1921.

During the Christmas season, 1921, Elizabeth and Bertha are living in Los Angeles, studying painting and sight-seeing. Poinsettias bloom in both their front and back yards, as they proudly report in letters to the family enduring a wintry Iowa. On New Year's Day they will be observing the Rose Festival in Pasadena. Instead of feeling depressed over finding themselves outside the traditional family enclosure at Christmastime, they savor their freedom. Back home, arrangements have changed drastically. Their parents' retirement house in Remsen, not the farm, is their abode. Both brothers—my father, Henry, and Uncle Jack—having married the two Lang sisters the previous year, are now parents of boys only a few months apart in age. "How are you, Lizzie, & little Donald?" Elizabeth writes. "I hope you both are fine . . . I bet it keeps you busy, Carrie, washing for two babies. Now you have an idea what twins would be like. Ha."

Bertha says the West Coast is even more expensive than anticipated. "Send a draft or certified or cashier's check," she instructs (from funds due them—their farm rent money, most likely). The weather is a disappointment, too. Although the California climate was touted as being nearly perfect, there have been heavy rains and flooding. "Of course the natives say . . . it's very unusual. Ha—that's a real joke; everything is always unusual here. Ha."

Elizabeth offers a wryly amusing slant on Hollywood news: "Mary Pickford & Doug came home last Sat.; as they hadn't [informed] me they were coming, I didn't go down to meet them! They surely have two most elegant homes, one at Beverly Hills and another in Santa Monica. Well, I haven't starred in a picture yet, so haven't begun plans for an elegant house in the hills. Ha."

All of it seems a long way from the Iowa homestead. Yet Elizabeth makes the effort. "So Bobby can sit up all by himself. Bet he looks cute. What does Donald look like?—like Bobby when he was little? If they both start up, you'll surely have enough music. Won't need a phonograph." By such small talk she hopes to keep connected to the family and will eventually become an aunt who demonstrates repeatedly how much she cares. The Harvard Five-Foot shelf of classics arrived in our farmhouse just when I needed such reading; the set of Americana encyclopedias came from her, too—and stipends for college, for my older siblings.

Every summer vacation Elizabeth returned to stay with her parents and Bertha in Remsen. While in Iowa, she quickly inhabited her small-town, farm-girl self, although her snazzy new Ford, stylish clothes, and smart costume jewelry clearly attested to her quite different life elsewhere.

While we were growing up, Elizabeth lived in Detroit, farther east than the term "back East" implied, which for us meant the Turkey River region near the Mississippi. Detroit according to our atlas was definitely East, a region counter to the West, as the farm was in so many ways the opposite of the city. In the emerging automobile culture of America, which she embraced enthusiastically, Detroit was the place to be. She enrolled in evening courses at Wayne State in order to advance in teaching, and upon earning an M.A. in business and commerce received a promotion. When she revealed her salary—several thousand dollars—to Mother and Lizzie, it sounded enormous to us. We felt lucky to be the heirs of this rich aunt, especially on birthdays and at Christmas.

She kept physically fit by golfing; competed in and won contract bridge tournaments; subscribed to the Detroit Symphony series; attended touring theater shows (Helen Hayes and Katherine Cornell her favorites). She shopped in Hudson's department store or across the river in Canada, where bargains in imported Scottish woolens could be found.

Rarely did she speak to us home folks about her teaching, except to boast of her success in classroom discipline. She set stiff goals which stretched her students to the limit, complain though they did. Some pupils had never before been subjected to such an orderly routine, she said, particularly if they had recently arrived from the South. But Elizabeth had no doubt but that these ill-educated "woolly-headed" ones, as she called them, would fit in eventually and discover their freedom in an atmosphere of order.

Jewish girls were her out-and-out favorite students. She admired their drive and determination to reach the top, an attitude toward achievement similar to her own. This enthusiastic appraisal of Jews countered the casual anti-Semitic remarks we commonly heard: the Jewish merchants in Sioux City were said to be overly crafty; lawyers of that ilk, shysters. Even from our Lutheran pulpit, Jews were depicted as Christ-killers, Reverend gloating that they had been condemned to wander the face of the globe forever.

Elizabeth, to our minds, completely escaped the stereotypical old maid syndrome and illustrated the good life possible if we were diligent in our studies. Whenever she was in Remsen, the five or ten dollar bills in the church collection plate attested to what she could afford to give away. Her zest for new experiences, interest in travel, general optimism, and cheer set a standard for us to emulate. There's a fulcrum in life, she seemed to be saying. One can fall on the doubting, despairing side, where under the aspect of eternity everything is folly and nothing endures or matters. Or you can plump for the side where hope constantly refills itself, even if you don't know it's happening; here strength of will and determination to succeed count, and you cannot be stymied by any difficulty for long.

However, there was more to Elizabeth's life than my childish idea of it formed through glimpses caught when she returned to Remsen on vacation. In Detroit she lived in an apartment on West Warren Street shared with a fellow teacher named Ruth, who was also Elizabeth's boon companion in most of her activities there. Mention of Ruth crept into Elizabeth's talk increasingly as time went on—their golfing games, success in bridge tournaments, trips together to the South or East. Once I remember Ruth visiting Remsen (or do I only imagine it?): fair-haired and even-featured, somewhat stocky and athletic, a big smile; altogether a perfect companion for Elizabeth. They made a thoroughly compatible pair, living together for decades. Now, of course, I wonder about the nature of this intimacy. The so-called "Boston marriages" consisted of maiden ladies sharing beds. I have no way of knowing whether such was the case here. Modern presumptions and speculations can be so very wrong, in this area. I've read those breathy biographies filled with contemporary interpretations and conclusions about what *really* went on in lives exhumed. I am certain it's more difficult to know about years'-past intimate matters than today's psychological analyzing suggests. We tend to read contemporary sensibility into all of this. Nowadays our openness and too-ready disclosures of sexual details perhaps only screens what is still reclusive, for any truth can wear many disguises and some truths are more true than others. Like a series of Russian dolls, there's always one smaller and different inside—and seemingly no end to it.

When Ruth died of cancer Elizabeth was terribly shaken, completely broken up over it. The strain of caring for Ruth, in addition to keeping on with schoolwork, must have been a terrible burden. Now that it was finally over, Elizabeth could not face a cheery Christmas in Remsen with all of us, who wouldn't understand the depth of her mourning or fathom her sorrow. Instead, she spent her vacation in Williamsburg, Virginia, where she wrote us that she hoped the salubrious climate and peaceful atmosphere might help her recuperate and recover her strength. The Christmas presents she sent puzzled us no end: each received a copy of Rudolph Fleischer's book regarding the proper use of language, which he claimed was the key to success in every endeavor. We didn't know what to make of this peculiar gift and few of us bothered to read what he had to say. I found a number of copies still in the farmhouse attic and threw them out the window.

After Ruth's death, Elizabeth lived alone in Detroit during the school term, guarding her privacy. Once, a few years into my first marriage, I wrote asking if my wife and I could live in her flat for a couple of weeks. We had been invited to visit friends who owned a summer house on one of the Thousand Islands and needed to perch for a while between engagements. We promised to be so tidy that upon her return in late August from Remsen, she would hardly know we'd been there. No answer. We made other plans. Elizabeth's silent treatment was her way of showing that the brash proposal had been improper. She probably thought it indicated the influence of my new wife, who simply didn't know any better, not having been acquainted with our family very long.

Finally the teaching began to wear Elizabeth down. The students seemed intractable, less motivated, often ornery and rebellious. Her style of Germanic severeness in the classroom came under criticism from the principal, who was imbued with John Dewey philosophy that each pupil should have a say in the educational process, not merely submit to a dictum from the teacher's platform.

Elizabeth put in for a transfer to another school, which turned out to be mostly black, in a rough neighborhood. On vacations now she looked beat and spoke of retiring before long, but only after serving the necessary number of years to earn the highest possible pension. Not that her expenses upon retirement would be great, for she and Anne owned the Remsen house free of mortgage, plus eighty acres of cropland for yearly income, and local living costs were modest. But Elizabeth had promised herself a grand finale of a trip, which would cost several thousand dollars: an excursion by sea and overland to Spain's Alhambra, the Egyptian Nile sites, the Holy Land, and various historic places in Italy.

In the mid-1950s, with her teaching career at an end, she paid her trip deposit money, found a congenial friend from Remsen to journey with her, and completed all travel arrangements. Camera in hand and with many rolls of film, she recorded every aspect of the experience, particularly in the Holy Land. Elizabeth later relived this trip during slide-lecture engagements before women's clubs, men's service groups like Rotary and Lion's, and church assemblies. She would become locally famous for her articulate, informative show, successfully transforming northwestern Iowa into a movable classroom. During our final housecleaning, Lois and I came upon the metal container holding her slides and other paraphernalia of those illustrated talks; but they were not to survive our despoilage. What value they had was too much connected with the presence of

Elizabeth; she alone could make these images come alive and be meaningful. Now they were merely leavings whose time had gone. The retirement years turned into still another adventure. Elizabeth brought her talents for organizing and running things to all the bodies she felt needed such leadership—especially the Women's Club (she attended state conventions as a delegate), the American Legion Auxiliary, and the Ladies Aid. She also easily resumed old friendships among the women she had known off and on throughout her life; the same held true for her relationship with local men, now that considerations of possible romantic entanglement were a thing of the past.

As for religion, Elizabeth was a quiet, attentive participant in church services, even if the pastor perhaps didn't quite know as much of the Bible as *she* did or sinned with a few grammatical lapses. She believed in the institution itself and God who stood behind it; the rough edges she could forgive. I doubt she was ever much of a hidebound Lutheran of the Missouri Synod sort. At college she attended Baptist and Methodist churches, and most of her Greiman cousins belonged to various Protestant "reform" congregations. She appeared serene enough in faith to be prepared to meet her Maker, but what she truly believed she kept to herself.

Now she golfed regularly on local courses with country-club types and took her place among the set of leading families. She entertained at bridge, Anne doing the baking; delicious cookies and decorated cakes were served on their handpainted, translucent china, accompanied by elaborate napery.

A staunch Republican, Elizabeth may have been tempted to enter politics. But she was intolerant of organizational formalities and too abrupt and outspoken, even about her Grand Old Party. Though she loved wearing elephant pins around election time, Elizabeth knew better than to spout Republicanism to any of us New Deal Democrats. Sometimes she forgot herself, however. I once overheard her express surprise to Anne after discovering that their dentist, Dr. Figg, whom they idolized—a courteous, fine-looking gentleman—turned out to be a Democrat. "You'd think he'd have more sense!" she said.

Unlike many Republicans, Elizabeth did not compromise her principles and beliefs just because the Democrats passed some laws that took society in a wrong direction, toward eventual, complete

AUNT ANNE (third from the right) WITH HER WORTHINGTON, MINNESOTA, QUILTING CIRCLE. ELIZABETH IS ON THE FAR RIGHT. LATE 1950s.

socialism. For years her salary had been docked for Social Security contributions, but when the time came for her to receive benefits, she refused to participate. The Sioux City office kept sending her letters and papers to sign. They informed her that the money thus far accumulated, which she had not accepted in payments since reaching age sixty-five, would all be disbursed in a lump sum. She need only sign.

But Elizabeth would not. Finally a telephone call; a bureaucratic, patient voice saying, "You don't understand . . . " To which Elizabeth replied, "*You* don't understand! I have saved for my years of retirement. I do not need to have the government support me, nor do I approve of this socialism. People are getting the idea the government will care for them. They can be shiftless and not save a penny—and it won't matter. I tell you, that law is bad for a person's character, and I for one will have nothing to do with it."

Somewhat taken aback, the voice on the other end of the line reasoned softly: the Medicare feature might be particularly important for an older person, since nobody knows when illness or a crippling disability might strike. Have you thought of that? "Indeed I have. I do not need the government to pay my doctor bills. Such a system is corrupting for doctors as well. Imagine! Paid for by the government instead of by the patient! Unless some of us speak out, these socialistic laws will stand, and the country will soon go down the drain." Finally the federal authorities gave up on her.

During the 1960s Washington was providing matching funds for communities interested in erecting libraries. But Elizabeth, who served on the Remsen library board and even headed it for a time, refused to apply for such a grant. "If we don't care enough about having a new library to pay for it all ourselves, we don't deserve it." Others felt the town should not allow this opportunity to pass and they overruled her. Just this once, they didn't see how taking federal cash would compromise them so badly; to ignore the offer would be like failing to pick up found money. "Don't you see?" Elizabeth replied. "Next the government will be telling us what books to *put in* the library. Once the government starts controlling what we read, we're living in a dictatorship, like Russia."

Oh, come come, Elizabeth, they objected, that's carrying the argument too far. What would be the harm? Not only could Remsen have a new library building, but we'll have to think of an appropriate name for it. Some are suggesting we name it for Curtis, since he's written books.

That did it. She resigned from the library board and watched indignantly as the new brick structure went up. When the time came to decide on the name business, she could still pull a few strings among friends, who mollified her now and hoped she wouldn't have hard feelings about their earnest efforts on behalf of the community. They knew better than to mention my books to her, for Elizabeth resented what she saw as portraits of herself and other family members in my creations and preferred not to be reminded of her displeasure. When I had proudly sent her an early copy of my first novel, I was somehow under the delusion that my art had completely changed everything and nothing recognizable remained. She informed me differently by return mail. "I got the book you sent. I didn't like it—not one bit—not any of it."

A good, crushing lesson for me to learn early on. However, she got over her ire, and I soon dismissed it from my mind.

Elizabeth wasn't always so negative about my career. Some years earlier, after my first marriage broke up and I accepted a teaching assignment in Tabriz, Iran, she enthusiastically backed my plans. She remarked that travel in difficult places was best done while young, and she was sorry she hadn't seen more of the world; she'd waited too long to go abroad. She rightly predicted the experience would change my life. And so later, in the mid-1960s when I wrote about my time there in *Persian Lions, Persian Lambs,* I dedicated the book to her; and she was pleased.

As "Aunt Eliza-buff" to her great nephews, she found her Sunday dinner-table place at Lois and Rex's. She and Jack would drive down for the day after church services, eat a big noon meal, talk in desultory fashion for a time, and perhaps inspect Lois's garden; there was the *Des Moines Register* and *Sioux City Journal* to peruse, and football on television to send her off in a snooze. In those years of the sixties and seventies after Anne's death, she tried to continue her program of activities, but at last she no longer felt capable of driving and thereby lost her vital mobility. She kept the car (a well-preserved Mercury) in the garage, however—wouldn't sell it—as if one day the process of aging might be reversed, and finding her faculties restored, she would be ready to drive off.

Early in the seventies, when I'd sometimes not see her for a year or more, I'd note how much she had "failed" (though the teacher in her would rise up to protest such a term). Less attentive, harder of hearing—despite her attempts to remain alert and quick—always making the effort to keep up and offering her bright smile. "Oh, must have dropped off a minute, ha! What were you saying?" When actually she'd been asleep there for half an hour. Now she was old, but the thrust of her personality still reinforced her brittle bones and held up her sagging skin; her eyes were as sky blue as ever. This woman was all of a piece. In her beginning was her end; she had made a life.

Lois confided to me that Elizabeth really shouldn't be living alone in her state. "I think she's had a few little strokes already." Aside from a couple of homebound phone friends, who checked in with her daily, Elizabeth had little backup support, no cleaning person who came by on a regular basis, nobody but Jack. "And Dad can hardly be expected to be responsible for her; he can barely keep going himself. But what can I do about it? I know for sure a nursing home is out of the question."

"Nobody could ever tell Elizabeth what she should do."

"She would never listen to anybody—and won't now."

Luckily, her death came suitably at once, with a massive stroke at age eighty-six. There was no messy health care situation for her to inflict on anybody. She went out with the capable efficiency she always expected of herself. But surprisingly, her affairs were in a careless condition. No last will could be found for some time. Every page of every book in the house had to be turned over for bills stashed away; and the family couldn't locate her recent IRS returns, which she made a point of figuring out and filing herself.

Jack rose to the demands of the occasion with renewed vigor. Now the stucco retirement house—and the one next to it, purchased by Grandfather for rental income—needed to be emptied and sold. Elizabeth had often expressed a wish that no household-goods sale be conducted on the lawn, with the subsequent indignity of having her belongings exposed to scrutiny. Nor should strangers snoop through her drawers in the house, open closets, or poke around the way they did when someone died and accumulated effects had to be disposed of. So, Jack, who had inherited everything, enjoyed a posture of largess and handed out the belongings of Bertha, Elizabeth, and Anne to anybody who expressed an interest. In those heady, complicated days, he somewhat forgot the rest of the family. There may have been items Lois would have liked, but he didn't think to ask her and she was too polite to speak up. Finally, what personal goods were left Jack stored in the farmhouse front parlor, where he hoped to spend weeks and months sorting through it. Not that he got very far with the monumental task. A lot remained for us to do.

Among Elizabeth's memorabilia was a photograph album of her year in Hurley, South Dakota. Since she appears in many of the pictures, I think Bertha snapped most of them while visiting in the

ELIZABETH, (back row, far right)
ON AN OUTING IN SOUTH DAKOTA, 1914.

spring of 1913. Empty streets and a wide sky; new-looking, false-front stores; the big brick high school with tall, narrow windows; groups of straggly pupils; scenes of horseplay—one in which two girls are inside a single pair of man's overalls; another with girls dressed in funny hats, moustaches penciled above their lips; a picnic gathering and there's young Elizabeth with her undershot jaw, the lower half of her face slightly dislocated (as it is with me), her sandy-colored hair neatly coiffed, a big smile.

I can imagine her explaining this photo-scrapbook to me, with its cartoon postcards, coy valentines, and paper mementoes, in a voice filled with bright urgency to convey to me the importance of life in a world still so fresh. For Elizabeth this was quite a special year, and the pictures give it a valuable dimension. I take on a self-consciousness she never would have in the telling. The record is here for anyone to see: these—her friends—Etta, Florence, all of them; the shutter open on a moment that seemed utterly modern. I relish the simple honesty exhibited in these pictures: the stripped quality of open frontier life, an absence of any awareness on the part of the subjects that the delineations are stark.

Of course, looking at photos of her there in Hurley I realize she does not yet know she will never marry. See those bachelors in ill-fitting hats and too short trousers lounging on the steps of the porch of what may be Elizabeth's boarding house? They *are* rather ridiculous-looking and no doubt she disdains their attentions. But they represent untaken chances for her to become a housewife, have children. However, perhaps she knew fully what she was doing all along and sensed that her life would not unfold in that fashion. She may have figured the choices would keep coming without limit and was never bothered by missed opportunities. She typified the optimism of the time—and why not? Her homesteading father had achieved comfortable burgher status and monetary success by hard work and the good sense to make the effort at a propitious time. Perhaps Grandfather's record inspired in her the comfortable notion of the endlessly favorable mutability of life.

Now the pictures tell a dead story, not her life's tale. And just a moment of that. They are arrayed before me like hard, fixed impressions stamped out of a living experience; awful footprints in a way, tracking across her days. I might be tempted to think they tell a sad tale of hopes missed; that her youthful fun is over. This young girl-teacher is wiser now, but wiser or not, she'll never have a chance to ameliorate anything that happened.

Yes, I can imagine Elizabeth picking up this photo album and turning the pages with a wondering look, for so many additional images would follow later, so many other people, other places. Her life has changed and grown so different that it would be hard for her to answer me if I asked, Who are those, in the pictures? The only one she recognizes is herself.

Don't I look funny in that awful dress? Boy, was I green!

THIS STRANGER IN UNIFORM

In the attic we unearthed several bundles of envelopes neatly tied with household string. All had been franked with "Free" scribbled in the upper right-hand corner. I recognized my childishly open handwriting, knew this was correspondence from my hitch in the Navy. Evidently Mother had saved every single scrap I wrote.

"You'll know what to do with *these,*" Lois said with a smile, handing them over.

Here was a diary of sorts, more complete than Bertha's or Elizabeth's; a record of activities over a period of many months. However, in addressing Mother (Lizzie and Jack too), I filter and edit what I relate. I will have to understand the nature of this "control" in order to reach behind the words. Until reading these letters, I had the notion of a seamless self, undergoing changes through the years but remaining essentially the same. Not true. This kid is a stranger to me.

As a stringy, nervous seventeen-year-old during freshman year at Grinnell, I kept a wary eye on news from the battlefields. My heady, wildly happy college existence seemed enhanced because of the termination looming, perhaps even an end to my life. I bonded easily with new friends, as if waiting all these years to meet up with them. My roommate, Stu, from Lombard, Illinois, was uncannily my precise age; we'd been born at almost the same hour. He and I and a few others among the 20 males on campus, finding ourselves among 250 women, immediately became BMOCs (big men on campus). We felt compelled to keep the college alive, particularly the extracurricular activities, until normal times returned. I worked on the newspaper, literary magazine, yearbook; helped out at weekly chapel (even delivering a sermon once); ran campus politics; trained to compete in track at the Drake Relays (no regular collegiate sports

I DRESSED AS LITTLE LORD FAUNTLEROY
DURING HAZING AT GRINNELL COLLEGE,
FALL 1944.

were carried on, for there were scarcely enough able-bodied men even
for basketball); enjoyed the novelty of naked phys. ed. swimming,
tangling like puppies in water volleyball contests, then returning to
the men's dorm with towels around our wet heads to dress quickly
and sing for the women in dining hall fests. I loved college
life—intensely sweet because it was played out against headlines on
the bombing of London, the siege of Stalingrad, and the landings at

Omaha Beach.

I had conquered shyness in public speaking by taking Professor Ryan's speech class and stepping to the podium whenever possible. I would surmount Victorian prudery and religious strictures concerning sex by also actively doing it one of these days. And full maturity meant I would have to join the war. I tried to think of my upcoming induction as a resolution of a long postponement. No beautiful time such as I was having could last forever.

Every generation had its war and this was mine. However, I'd been born a bit late to qualify in the age set I felt part of; possibly I'd be left out unless I scrambled to be with them in their significant hour, the one against which they would measure themselves the rest of their days. Those younger than me would be of a totally different time; not knowing the Depression or World War II, their lives would be shaped by influences about which I could only speculate. I would not belong to that generation group; nor would they have me. My lot was with those undergoing *this* war, and somehow I would have to join up before the fighting ended. Ironically, in later years my having been a serviceman in World War II would often be greeted with incredulity, because in our family the aging clock ran behind time and none of us showed much gray hair until well past sixty. My youthful exterior belied inner notions of the period I identified with, what generation I was.

June, 1945: My eighteenth birthday was approaching and draft registration—followed no doubt by a quick call-up from the Army unless I enlisted in the Navy, as planned. Though the European war was mostly over, I might still find myself in the war against Japan. But since hostilities in the Pacific also seemed to be winding down, my military role might be slight. However, I would qualify for a lame-duck button upon discharge and receive benefits under the GI Bill of Rights, which I needed in order to continue college. My education fund, that legacy from my dead father, had been largely exhausted during freshman year.

Final farewells at Grinnell throbbed with emotion, scored to theme music from films like *Mrs. Miniver* and *The White Cliffs of Dover.* At Christmas I had been in love with Ginger; now it was blonde Ruthie from Chicago, a hockey girl with big calves (though I'd not felt them), who had a poetic way with language and promised to take me walking one day in her favorite haunts in Jackson Park on the South Side, where we would feed the ducks and stroll among flowering shrubs. There were last-minute blanket parties at Arbor Lake, petting that went only so far, while the portable radio played "I'll get by . . . as long as I have you."

At the Navy recruitment center in Des Moines I flunked the physical—a high level of albumen in my urine. They told me to go home. There, family concern over my health, remembering that my father died at thirty-six, became mixed with sympathy over my disappointment. If I didn't join the armed services, what would I do? The scholarship to Grinnell might be renewed, though my grades hadn't been high. Possibly extra funds to continue could be found somewhere—from Aunt Elizabeth?

I hated the idea of showing up for classes in the fall. "What happened? What're *you* doing back?" Legionnaire Uncle Jack seemed somewhat embarrassed over my poor showing. Ours was a family that sent sons to war; Donald had already been killed because of it. Of course, Mother would happily have me 4-F and safe, but she knew better than to voice such feelings.

When our physician found nothing wrong with my urine, I decided to take the Navy physical again and boarded the train, switching at Fort Dodge to an interurban electric carriage that scooted noiselessly through the cornfields and ended up in Des Moines. Following the tip of a fellow enlistee, I gulped about a quart of water in order to thin myself out. The lab sample I peed for them was very, very pale. To my great relief, I passed. Inland Midwestern boys have always been ocean-hungry and traditionally make up a good portion of the fleet. The Navy offered the prospect of clean ship's quarters and varied ports of call, though I knew from brother Ken's V-letters from Guam, a sailor could also end up stationed on an island hellhole. And yet, if I had not made it into the Navy, the Army would have taken me promptly, with no to-do about the physical. After basic, I would have been shipped to the jungles of the South Pacific, which had already done in my oldest brother, now recuperating in a hospital near Los Angeles.

In the cavernous Des Moines examination room of the Navy center, we future gobs stood naked before Uncle Sam—the ultimate father figure, as Uncle Jack had conditioned me to think. Over half the recruits were blacks, whose gleaming, dusky bodies were a complete novelty to me. None lived in the farm country of northwest

Iowa. Although we sometimes encountered them on Sioux City streets, as well as Indians from the South Sioux City reservation, we didn't think much about them. We caught the local attitude: We have our world, they have theirs.

A couple of black families lived in Grinnell, and one boy, Tibbs, who wasn't in the service for some reason, took courses at the college. A "townie," he was affiliated with our dormitory and would appear for Monday night house meetings. Tibbs was designated the upperclassman I was to serve in the hazing rituals still in effect then; I would carry out his wishes, run errands, clean up. But he asked nothing of me. According to the rules, I must purchase an oak cricket paddle, jigsawed at the lumber company, then paint his name on it under a Maltese cross, symbol of the college. At a special fall house meeting, the climax of "hell week" initiation, each freshman presented an upperclassman with a decorated paddle, the gift to be acknowledged with a whack across the freshman's buttocks. Tibbs looked acutely embarrassed when I handed him the cricket bat. Even in egalitarian Grinnell, whose founder J. B. Grinnell had housed and befriended John Brown and actively aided the Underground Railroad, a black did not feel comfortable having a white boy bend over, left hand on ankle, right one cupping testicles, inviting the degradation of a beating. Tibbs swatted me lightly to get it over with, but the other sadistic upperclassmen roared and egged him on to do it again, harder, harder—until a wallop broke the bat and splinters flew everywhere.

Now in the Navy lineup I eyed the dark, unfamiliar bodies, naked alongside me. As they bent over and spread cheeks for the anal inspection by white doctors, they were reversing the role of Tibbs and me in the Grinnell hazing. In 1945 few of these Lincoln High and North High Des Moines blacks had yet become alert to demands for racial equality that would grip them a decade later. A cowed bunch, they looked more scared than me, though now we were on a par in this situation.

When the physical examination was over, we were ordered to dress, allowed to regain our dignity, for clearly the Navy didn't want either black or white recruits to raise their right hands and pledge allegiance while unclothed and helplessly vulnerable.

On the troop train to Chicago I sat up all night in a brightly lit, crowded coach, unable to sleep, intensely excited. I didn't want to miss any of this adventure, weary though I was. The meandering route through small towns not served by the major trunk lines baffled me—as if this circuitous path were necessary to avoid Stuka dive bombers. At dawn the suburbs of Chicago appeared, commuters with their newspapers waiting on platforms. But we did not stop, merely rocked on past slowly, a heavy load of war, somberly reminding them that the national effort still continued, the enemies of America needed to be defeated, and some young men like us would be killed. The names of these towns which suddenly materialized after miles of cornfields, one village blending into the next, seemed glamorous because my college friends had talked of them so often. Des Plaines, Riverside, Oak Park . . . here was the beginning of the great city at last. All my life I'd yearned for Chicago. How keen my disappointment had been when told I wasn't old enough to ride along with the others to the Chicago World's Fair of 1933. Now I'd finally made it; at the first opportunity on liberty, I would explore the streets, cover the North and South sides, take boat rides on Lake Michigan. I longed to walk down Chicago's gritty avenues and roam the ethnic sections, precisely because everything about the city would be so different from rural Iowa.

I was ready for the abstraction urban life embodied, for I had grown up familiar with the basic underpinnings of life that city dwellers no longer thought about—such as that bottled milk originally came from a cow and that the Chicago commodities exchange dealt in futures representing tons of actual grain that would one day be in storage somewhere. City people could ignore farm fundamentals and live many removes from the living shoot and budding fruit—all those first stages of life I knew so well. Urban complexity would challenge my intellectual growth. It was a natural development after years on the farm.

Tuesday night, July 24, 1945

Dear Mother,

This morning we drilled for three hours with rifles. We learned the manual of arms, etc. Wow! is it hot up here! This afternoon it was 100° in the shade. A couple of guys fainted from the heat. When it gets this hot we're allowed to wear just our skivvy shirts—not our jumpers, but that doesn't help much.

Today we got a stripe sewed onto our jumpers. That

means we aren't new boots anymore, and we have only 58 more days of boot training.

I was assigned to Camp Moffit, our company housed in a building designated by letter—not because they hadn't gotten around to naming the barracks shaped like an airplane hanger (others like huge chicken houses) but as part of the master scheme to depersonalize us as quickly as possible, make us fit for killing the enemy. Or being killed, if things came to that, without making a fuss about it. The uniformity of clothing issued, though we were so different in sizes, emphasized our sameness; none of the garments fit anyone. However, I couldn't fault the quality. The shoes were well made, the skivvies strong at the seams, the white cotton uniforms tightly woven and capable of withstanding many bleached washings. Later, when issued a blue pea jacket of deep piled wool, I would have a garment (though short in the sleeves) that would linger in my wardrobe for decades, perfect for winter nights in Saratoga Springs. Whenever I pulled it on, I recalled that we once had a government so insistent on quality that it provided gear like this for its fighting men.

Given my college background and typing skills, I was appointed company clerk, a station which accorded me special privileges and a working relationship with the C.O., a petty officer who had been a professional baseball player in civilian life and looked like actor Robert Preston.

Tuesday night, July 31, 1945

Dear Mom,

... Yesterday started our first of the work week, and 85 of our men were down in the chow hall. Keeping track of whether all the men were there and at their right stations was bad enough, but I also had to send replacements for those who went to sick bay or dropped by the wayside. Today was terribly hot—110° in the chow hall—thank God I wasn't there except to dash in and out ...

This morning I had a date with a Wave, and I had another date this afternoon. I had to bring some war bond applications over to the hostess' house, and while she checked them all we had cokes and a nice visit. She was the first woman I've talked to in three weeks, and she wasn't bad-looking, either. I had to bring some more applications over this afternoon, so I went through the same procedure. There are things about this clerk's job that aren't so bad . . .

In correspondence home throughout my Navy stint, I don't miss a chance to describe my successes, particularly with the girls, careful to limn in a picture Mother would like to have of me. Since her operation for bowel cancer five years before and the stroke during surgery which paralyzed her arm and slurred her speech, she was a semi-invalid—more in attitude than physically, as time went on. For her the great struggle to rear us was over. She would sit near the radiator in the dining room, an afghan over her legs, an unread book in her lap, while Lizzie took over house management and cared for her older sister, gaining the ascendancy. I felt it my duty to let Mother know that her hardships had been worth it; the life she had given me and shaped according to her principles was proceeding splendidly. It would please her to know I was enjoying myself, each triumph I mentioned intended as proof.

The six-week training period, designed to squash the crybaby out of us, toughened our bodies. We learned skills that would probably be of no use (tying various rope knots; shooting a target), and most of our lingering individuality evaporated. Personal possessions were reduced to what could be contained in a small canvas bag, which might be inspected any time, clothing tightly rolled. The three-tier bunk was our only home spot—a simple pallet, an area that was "ours." No privacy was possible even there, since the next guy lay twelve inches away, his pillow on the other end. Only when the lights-out curfew plunged the barracks into darkness and silence (after a few catcalls and yelps) could one's reflections well up. That would last only a minute or two, however, because sleep overcame us almost instantly, we were so exhausted. The next thing we knew, hearty guards were shouting "Drop your cocks and grab your socks," as we were chivied awake by reveille whistle-blowing—a horrible, abrasive, instant mayhem and the start of another dreadful day. But I felt tough and clean, with nocturnal emissions easing sexual tensions and not even much chance to think about that department.

My letters home were about none of the above.

Aug. 8, 1945

Dear Mother,
    . . . We're now on a regular schedule of classes and drill,

etc., and the time is going faster. Today I got my "pussy-stripes"—three of them. I'm apprentice petty officer first class. Our certificates will be made out later. We got our "floating fives" today, too. [Payday] I was getting a little low.

Our second haircut was today, and I timed mine. It was exactly 40 seconds from the time I stepped in that chair till the time I stepped out. That's really shearing!

I have to sew on my stripes tonight, yet, so I'd better close. We're having our company picture taken tomorrow, so I have to have my full rigging on.

The weather is nice and cool, and I'm having a good time.

Love,
Curt

P.S. Wasn't that swell about Russia declaring war on Japan? What do you think of the atomic bomb?

What indeed? The front page of the *Chicago Tribune* pictured the blast in color as if it were a pretty thing, but I felt a foreboding I'm not reading into it now, these many years later. Events were moving fast—too fast—while I remained stuck in boot camp.

I could survive this tough life. In a perverse way I began to feel satisfaction over the dehumanization process: just a cog in the machine of war, the whole company more of an entity than any single person. In my niche as clerk I was neither in danger of rolling around on the bottom with the misfits and weaklings, nor was I among the brawny leaders who gloried in this return to an animal state. I didn't care to get too close to those bozos. Because of my years of solitary farm life, I hadn't known for sure if I would be able to join the herd, which I'd have to in the cities of my future, moving among various people in a close mix. Now I knew I could.

V-J Day, Aug. 15, 1945

Dear Mother,

It's a great day, even up here at Great Lakes. Last night when the news was announced, bells rang, sirens blew, and everything was bedlam. Then two companies out of our battalion were chosen to march down State Street in Chicago today. We were all a little disappointed our company wasn't picked.

All schedules for today have been cancelled, and it's just

AT BOOT CAMP,
GREAT LAKES NAVAL TRAINING CENTER,
SUMMER 1945.

like Sunday. We even slept till 6:00 this morning. At 9:30 we
have church services outdoors. All the Protestants in the Green
Bay area form on one drill field, and all the Catholics form on
another. There'll probably be about 30,000 boots, and it should
be quite impressive.

   . . . The big parade is forming now, and I'll have to fall
out.

Love,
Curt

But in the hullabaloo over the end of the war, I would still manage to be a victim of it, in a way. Scarlet fever was spreading in some barracks. As a child I'd been vaccinated when the serum was first developed, experimentally, but I had not completed all the shots. Perhaps because I was partially immunized, when I contracted the disease I had only a mild fever and headache and didn't turn myself in at sick bay for a couple of days—until a rash appeared on my stomach.

I have pondered this episode, trying to understand my psychological makeup at the time. While a success at conventional manliness, I suddenly succumbed to weakness and perhaps sought a way out. Of course, I did catch the actual scarlet fever bug. But I may have gone out to meet it, opening myself to a way of being saved from the hellish heat of the macadam drill fields in August, the grueling routines, seamen to the right and left keeling over and lying there, troops marching around the fallen bodies with averted eyes and steeled indifference.

At sick bay my tongue's color and stomach rash confirmed the orderly's suspicions: another case of scarlet fever. An ambulance was ordered up immediately.

But I can walk! Got over here to sick bay, didn't I?

Nevertheless, I was placed on a stretcher and shoved into the ambulance. Lights flashing, siren whooping, I was whisked through the Great Lakes Naval Training Center, past the parade grounds with white-garbed sailors in orderly squared formations. Off to the contagious ward of the hospital.

Fortunately, I wasn't billeted near maimed victims recuperating from war wounds—*that* would have made me too much of an imposter. In my feverish head the atom bomb, end of the war, and victory celebrations all got rather mixed up. I took on the role of having been stricken in the service of my country, perhaps a hero of a lesser sort, but still valiant. By some miracle I had avoided a testing under battlefire for my red badge of courage and could take a well-earned rest, opting out of conflict with my honor in tact.

17 Aug. 1945

Dear Mother,

You never know what's going to happen next. I'm in the hospital with scarlet fever. I won't be able to write anything but postcards for the next 21 days because letters carry germs.

Of course, I'll lose my company clerk's job, etc., but I'd lose that anyway when I got out of boot. All yesterday morning I instructed my assistant about what had to be done, so I guess things aren't in too much of a mess.

By the way, it's true when they say the Navy gives the best medical care in the world. They really treat us good.

Love,

Curt

My company of buddies would complete training without me (who were they?—not one do I remember). After boot camp, following the regulation home leave, they would be shipped to the Pacific in order to relieve long-term sailors eager for discharge. They would fill in the destiny intended for me, but which I had circumvented.

In a few days, having scarcely a blush of scarlet rash and almost no fever, I was given no more penicillin shots. "Some guys have had over 100 . . . As long as I stay healthy I won't get any." Jim to my left, from Muskegon, Michigan, and Bob to my right, a coal miner's son from Centralia, Illinois, were not reflective types; they lay bored and miserable, not sick enough to relax into bed care and not well either. Each morning they'd get their shots in the ass; "Sunny-side up!" the nurse would call cheerfully, needle extended as she approached. There was almost something sexy about it. Our favorite was a small, pretty blonde with a fun-loving directness. We kept reminding one another of the officer/enlisted man barrier, knew we must not be outrageously fresh with her. Impudence might not merely be slapped down; we could be hauled up on charges of disrespect for an officer if she decided to get mean about it. The nurse relished the bind we were in, enjoying the flirting but also the power she had over us. Jim never awoke before she was right there, waving the needle, pulling down his sheet, and when she'd see his usual morning state, slam the needle into him rougher than necessary, saying "Hey, what's this? You're supposed to be sick."

Red Cross ladies toured the ward, spreading cheer among us, passing out stationery, pencils, fruit, and books. I helped myself to my first Trollope, *Barchester Towers,* plus a good supply of contemporary trash. "Today I read *Of Mice and Men* by Steinbeck,"

I wrote Lizzie. "It wasn't very good." By which I meant *she* wouldn't like it—all that odd business with the soft-headed guy. "Now I'm starting *Cimarron* by Edna Ferber." More the sort of novel she read to us aloud those long, snowy winter evenings of our childhood.

> Sept. 2, 1945
>
> Dear Mother,
>   Today I learned that I might have a heart murmur. The doctor checked me thoroughly, but wasn't quite sure. Probably tomorrow they'll give me an electrocardiogram test . . . In the meantime I'm a bed patient again . . . If I do have a heart murmur, I'll be moved to the rheumatic ward for complete rest. I could get over it in a few weeks . . .

A slight heart murmur would not be reason enough to prevent me from going back to active duty. The chief doctor told me to "get up, put on my clothes, and walk around," and the next day he promised to rule on what should be done with me. I didn't want a medical discharge, for it would seem a kind of failure.

He decided I should go back to boot camp. "It was very nice getting into my whites again after 23 days of these pajamas." Now that the flip of destiny had decided things, I would make the best of it. Having just received a five-dollar bill from Jack in the mail, I happily described food orgies in the canteen: "lots of ice cream sundaes lately, and they're surely good in this hot weather."

"Three more out of our ward were classified as rheumatic patients today. I guess I really was lucky to get out of it. This is mainly a Marine hospital, it seems. You see them limping around, or without arms or legs, and big scars on their heads. You certainly can see that there's been a war on, in this place." And my dubious habitation here is not in the same category. I have lost ten pounds because of poor appetite and little exercise. "You don't get very hungry just lying in bed. Of course, I'm not thin. I weigh about the same as I did when I left home, but I had gained in boot camp."

With the summer ended, the war over, just how would I finesse my future? Early separation out would mean little college time on the GI Bill; therefore, my strategy (if I were to have a choice) should be to remain in the Navy as long as possible. With no danger of getting killed in battle, why not enjoy a full tour as a paid employee of the

U.S. government?

I didn't try to settle in with the new boot company to which I was assigned. "I'm on light duty till Saturday, so don't drill or go to PT classes. This morning the company is drilling, and I'm writing letters; this is a nice way to go through boot camp. I'll only have three and a half working days till we leave." I'm clearly acquiring a talent for goldbricking. Eventually I'd receive liberty time, enough to make it home for a few days.

Sept. 20, 1945

Yesterday I had a lot of fun with 50 clb. machine-gun practice. I'll have to tell you about it when I get home. The gun is electrically controlled, just the size of a regular gun, and we fire tracers at planes on a screen. It's on the same principle as the penny arcade machine gun, but much more realistic, with sound and all.

Last night I went to the technicolor movie "State Fair." It was supposed to take place at the Iowa State Fair. It was a beautiful show and very good. I hope you all get to see it. Lizzie, Jack, and Lois will probably be reminded of the time we went. The parking place where we pitched the tent is even represented.

I'll be in Sioux City a week from tonight. Until then . . .

Love,
Curt

Once again my letter-writing voice cozens the home folks readers, telling not what I feel but rather what their notion of my reactions should be. I was right in thinking they'd be thrilled by the glamour of having Hollywood pay attention to an event which had seemed to us strictly local. But that cotton-candy extravaganza disturbed me because of the way a glorious-looking falseness was projected as if it were true. *I* had been a farm boy at that Iowa fair, not the imposter on the screen. Jack, Lizzie, Lois, and I had camped out at the fairgrounds only the previous year. Everything I knew about rural life indicated the film was a lie. Of course, picture shows were mere entertainment, not artistically serious, the way a book might be. Mostly movies were not expected to be about anything one knew, which made gaudy *State Fair* particularly offensive.

Nobody in the audience seemed to mind the fakery; in fact, they were taken in by it. "It's just a show," a buddy remarked, when I groused a little too much. Perhaps I deplored the movie so vehemently because already I had some intimation that one day, in my writings, I would attempt to get the picture right.

The short pass for a home visit, before my orders came through, might be the last for months if they shipped me to the Pacific. That week on the farm has disappeared from recall, maybe because I was returning to a shaped self of earlier years, my growing adulthood momentarily on hold. For a few days I foraged deeply into the territory of my youth, packing it in for the times ahead when I'd be far away. No doubt the tale of my life, as I related it to the adults at home, was altered to fit the expected pattern, the outline known to all of us without having to speak of it. It was too late for any serious advice from the home folks—opinions that might seem to pressure me to do this or that. Their input had come earlier; now they were merely background for me to play out my days against.

I routed my return to Great Lakes by way of Grinnell, in order to visit friends and lay the groundwork for my eventual return. I expected to try for another scholarship, perhaps wait tables in the cafeteria or clerk in the bookstore as my friends did, employment as such having social cachet. All the campus big shots seemed to be scholarship students. Since Grinnell did not allow automobiles and nobody sported expensive wardrobes, there were few ways to show wealth. Those who came from rich parents kept quiet about it, hoping their home addresses—Winnetka, Edina, Scarsdale—in the school directory wouldn't give them away. This was a college milieu perfect for me, and I was determined to get back into Grinnell somehow.

Oct. 7, 1945

Dear Mother,
    This will be just a short letter to let you know I'm all right and shipping out tomorrow for Navy Pier in Chicago. The ship I'll be on is in dry dock there, and I expect to be scraping paint and tearing down the flat top, which was used to train Navy fliers and is now going to be turned back to the steamship line which owned it, and I imagine we'll have to get it in shape . . .

With a half dozen other sailors, I had been singled out to report to the *U.S.S. Sable* in Port Chicago. But Chicago hardly seemed a

HOME ON LIBERTY,
WITH LIZZIE (on left) AND MOTHER (on right),
NOVEMBER 1945.

real port (this was before St. Lawrence Seaway opened the Midwest to world shipping). The *Sable* was a converted Mississippi River paddle steamer, over which a flat deck had been built; Navy fliers practiced here before being assigned to carriers. Now it was not in dry dock but moored permanently to the pier. The training planes were gone by the time I walked up the gangplank, but a glance at the flight deck told me it was awfully short for a runway. Yes, we heard, several planes had crashed, the pilots killed. But it was wartime, and the accidents had been hushed up. The Navy and other branches could sometimes be cavalier about the safety of their troops in wartime—as perhaps the Air Force had been with Cousin Don, killed in a collision over Phoenix, Arizona. And whose fault? Nobody would say.

Oct. 9, 1945

Dear Mom,

I'm a real sailor now. I'm living in the bow of this baby flattop, which is 580 feet long . . .

My duties consist of washing the deck, polishing, and other light maintenance work . . . The draft of men we're replacing hasn't left yet.

We only expect to be on here for a month, and then Henry Ford will probably buy it to use for a car transport. We may sail to Cleveland or New York after the ship is sold. Frankly, I doubt if it could make the voyage—it's a pretty old tub. Just the same, it was pretty thrilling to walk up the gangplank with our sea bags over our shoulders . . .

The chow is wonderful! All the milk you can drink; thick, juicy steaks; fresh fried eggs; all the very best food.

A laundry washes all our clothes for nothing, a tailor shop presses and alters our clothes. We have lockers instead of sea bags for stowing our gear. Yes, I'm in heaven. I never knew the Navy could be like this.

Love,

Curt

Something strange about the activities aboard the *Sable*. What was the point of polishing brass and scrubbing decks, as if we were at sea, when the war was over? Of course, the dismantling of facilities created during the emergency took time. Perhaps this old training carrier just hadn't been gotten around to. In the meantime, maintenance must continue; somebody had to look after it. I shouldn't bother my head about why.

And I didn't. Many nights I would leave the ship, board the streetcar on Grand and head into the city, all transportation free, my destination usually the Servicemen's Center, where show tickets were available. Chicago would be mine at last.

October Something

Dear Mother,

The trouble with this going out every night is that I never get any letters written.

Thursday night my buddies and I really made a night of it. First we saw the movie "Love Letters" with Jennifer Jones, and it was very good. After the movie we went to the theater and

I HAD MY PICTURE TAKEN IN CHICAGO
WHILE A SEAMAN ON THE *U.S.S. SABLE,* 1945.

saw Elizabeth Bergner in "The Two Mrs. Carrolls." The play
was a good murder mystery and very well done. Although the
star is supposed to be the world's best actress and she *was* very
good, there really wasn't too much difference between it and a
high school or college play. Maybe that was because the play
itself wasn't so well written compared to the actors who played
in it.

Again I try to accommodate Mother's sensibilities; she should not
feel left out because cultural experiences are available to me but not
to her. I go on to report looking up "Greenie," a Le Mars classmate
now in nurse's training at St. Luke's hospital, and tell of another day
of liberty which *began* at 8:30 A.M.

> I spent the entire morning in the Art Institute of Chicago. I
> planned to see the aquarium or museum but my feet were so
> tired that I went to a movie instead (free). It was a double
> feature and lasted four hours. I've just had supper here at the
> Servicemen's Center and have called Stringer twice [a former
> roommate of my sister Ruth], but she's not in. I'll try once
> more, else I'll go out with Greenie again tonight.
>   That in brief is what I've been doing lately.
>
>   Love,
>   Curt

I was on liberty so often because no regular work routine was
established on the *Sable.* Under a duty officer, I fulfilled some night
watches, but most of the ship's company seemed to be ashore. Some
of the officers, many of whom I'd never seen before, only showed up
on payday.

                                          Oct. 24, 1945
> Dear Mother,
>   . . . This is Wednesday afternoon, and I'm writing letters
> at the very nice Lutheran Servicemen's Center on Randolf St.
> It's much quieter and more "homey" than the huge 12-floor
> Chicago Center.

With the city beginning to overwhelm me, I retreat infantilely, a good Sunday School boy, and hang around with the Lutherans. Not quite able yet to take on everything out there. On Rush Street I'd patronized some pretty low dives and seen raunchy floor shows, while outside the door, girls with skimpy skirts and overly made-up faces hung around enticing sailors or anybody with cash. My initiation into the fleshpots seemed to be happening too fast.

> Later this afternoon a buddy and I are going to visit Field's
> Museum, and I'm expecting an interesting evening with Grinnell
> kids on the South Side tonight. I haven't been further south
> than the Illinois Central depot, but I don't suppose I'll get lost.
> The worst section of Chicago is between them and the Loop,
> but I'll be going almost all the way by subway so I don't expect
> to be beat up by a bunch of niggers.

Clearly, Tibbs hadn't swatted my ass quite hard enough.

Those Grinnell "kids" were actually graduates, women I'd known in their senior year, now holding jobs in Chicago and rooming together. On campus they had been like older sisters, my friend Stu and I serving as substitute men because their real guys were off at the battlefronts. They toyed with our attentions but never forgot we were only seventeen-year-old freshmen. Being seniors, they had no lockup hour at the dorm, so we could revel with them late into the night, feel the special privilege of being in their sophisticated company.

When I located the small apartment house where they now lived, the door below was locked. I hunted up the name tag and pushed the button next to it. I heard a funny guttural noise that stopped after a while. Tried the door but it held firmly. After several of these attempts, one of them finally came down to let me in, explaining what happened to the doorlock when they buzzed me back. So now I knew. One more notch to my city experience. Yes, I was wet behind the ears, but discomfort over it was soon forgotten.

Much of that year in Chicago I had a regular date every Monday night with these women. I'd help them clean the apartment, join in the cooking, listen to records, play bridge, or just talk. I was a bit in love with all of them, but with my emotions so dispersed and unfocused, nothing but casual kissing ever came of it. The obligation to be a serious lover was temporarily suspended, perhaps to my unconscious relief. They had no regular dates, for they were caught in the women-left-behind-the-lines syndrome.

Finally one Monday an Army captain showed up. He belonged to Sue or Ellen—one of them—and my puppy fun vanished. I felt ill at ease in an officer's company socially, though he was genial and courtly toward me. As the hour grew late, he and his girlfriend quietly slipped down the hall, entered a bedroom, and closed the door. I tried to keep the banter going to cover my embarrassment, but there was no way to hold our connection intact. My special, exclusive time with this houseful of attractive girls was over. The guys they'd been waiting for were coming home.

Oct. 26, 1945

Dear Mother,

If this letter looks awfully scribbly, it's because of a little accident I had yesterday. The end of my right forefinger got pinched under a barrel drum yesterday . . . The work has been extremely hard and long. Yesterday morning we carried heavy iron pipes and steel grates off the ship for three steady hours with no rest. The guy in charge is the worst slavedriver on the ship.

. . . We're leaving Monday—much sooner than I had expected. Temporarily we're going to Tower Hall in Chicago, which is a Shore Patrol barracks. From there we shall be shipped to a new assignment in a few days . . . The best rumor is that we'll be going to New York to join the Third Fleet for the world cruise. I certainly hope so . . .

Farewell to our enigmatic life aboard the gray, ghostly ship dead beside the pier, gangplank angled toward liberty in glittery Chicago and above us the arc light atop the Palmolive Building swooping around and around like Hollywood search lights on the evening of a premier.

I made the most of each remaining night in the city, spending one dancing at the Aragon.

Oct. 28, 1945

. . . The ballroom is a mammoth, ornate place patterned

after an open patio in Spain. Stars twinkle way up above and filmy clouds drift across the night sky. I would have sworn I was outdoors by that clever overhead. Of course, Henry King's orchestra was tops—he broadcasts every night at twelve over Chicago's largest station. It was fun being part of a broadcast.

After the dance we had an hour's ride back to the South Side, and then I had to come all the way back . . .

I'm on duty today, and have had an hour of good hard work carrying chains, lines, and buoys from the anchor room to the dock. That will probably be the last hard work I'll have to do aboard this ship. This afternoon I'll start packing, do a little washing (to get the hang of it again) and be ready to shove off after pay day tomorrow. I plan to send a money order home . . . because I'll have way too much cash on me.

Good-bye from the *Sable*. Next stop—Tower Hall, Chicago.

Love,
Curt

Before the Navy relinquished the *Sable* they offered the public an open house, beginning at 1:00 P.M. "I was on liberty at 10 (thank heavens) so wasn't overrun by the hundreds of people and little kids who were climbing all over the ship." The *Sable* and its sister ship, the *Wolverine,* docked one pier over, were the only large Navy ships in Port Chicago, so there was considerable local interest in them.

Next day at the decommissioning ceremony on the foredeck, which principally involved the lowering of the Stars and Stripes, an incredible (to me) array of officers were lined up in neat rows, from the captain to his phalanx of first and second lieutenants to a passel of ensigns and petty officers. I figured they must have rounded up all the brass in the area for the purpose of making a good last show, because the ritual of decommissioning had a holy air about it, almost like the desanctification of a church no longer to be used.

My final payday on the *Sable* yielded only nine dollars. "I guess they're taking out plenty for war bonds, so I won't be sending home any. I'll need all the cash I have if I'm in New York or San Francisco by this weekend." Meanwhile, at the transit "barracks," Tower Hall, life was remarkably cushy.

Oct. 29, 1945

Tower Hall is ideally situated just off Michigan Ave. near
the Palmolive Building. It's twenty stories high and I'm on the
thirteenth. Our bedding (two sheets, blankets, pillow, pillow
case, and towel) was issued to us for 25¢. We sleep on inner
spring mattresses in oak, doubledecker beds. The whole place
was a ritzy hotel before the war and little change has been made.

We have lounges with pool and ping pong tables, a classy
dining hall (not chow hall) with civilians serving . . . I haven't
the faintest idea what type of work I'll do here, how long I'll be
here, or if I'll be permanently assigned here. I know we'll be on
liberty practically all the time.

The first weekend of extended liberty, I planned to board the
Hiawatha and journey ten hours by rail to Sioux City, where the
folks would meet me at 10 P.M. Friday evening, returning me to catch
the noon train on Sunday—even though I had been home just a
couple of weeks before. I felt the need to get my bearings, Chicago
being too heady, though I explained, "It probably will be my last
chance before shipping out," hoping that my need to touch base
wouldn't seem regressive.

Upon return to Chicago, I tried to figure out what my life at
Tower Hall would be like.

Oct. 31, 1945

Dear Mother,

. . . Frankly, I haven't the faintest idea what in the heck
I'm doing here. It's sort of a rest home for vets returning from
overseas and awaiting discharge. I'm in temporary ship's
company in the Master at Arms department. I have duty every
fourth day. On that day I'm on watch for an eight hour period
to check liberty cards, patrol the halls, help in the main office,
or whatever it happens to be . . .

On the days you aren't on duty, you don't do anything at
all. There is no reveille, although we have to turn in our liberty
cards at muster at 8 A.M. Then we can go back to bed again and
sleep until liberty starts at one o'clock. In other words, we're on
liberty practically all the time. The food is very good, and we're
living in luxury. You've seen those cartoons, "This ain't the
Army." Well, "this ain't the Navy," either.

But what was it? The mystifying irregularity of the operation unsettled me; never had I heard so much scuttlebutt in explanation—none of it on the mark, as I learned years later. Certain floors were heavily secured with grates and padlocks; nobody entered these sealed-off areas and yet their entrances had to be guarded carefully. Companies of veteran sailors would arrive, then leave for discharge centers after a week or so.

The Servicemen's Center became my second home. I learned to bowl on a stage under bright lights but was puzzled by the cavernous, decayed-looking theater in the dark beyond us. Figured the Center must be in some dilapidated building nobody knew what else to do with. The ornate decorations were in such pitiful shape, I hardly bothered looking at them, though after a snooze in the music lounge I might wake up to see a caryatid staring at me or a gilded cupid in flight. I bowled quite regularly under the eyes of an absent audience out there in the shadows, never knowing that I was in the Auditorium, one of Chicago's most famous buildings of the Sullivan period of architecture, later faithfully restored to its early grandeur.

From the Center's windows I could observe the Chicago scene and report on it to the folks at home.

Nov. 19, 1945

... There was a big crowd of people, motorcycle cops and such, standing around the entrance of the Congress Hotel yesterday afternoon. I couldn't find out what was wrong so concluded they must be waiting to see some celebrity. Pretty soon a cab drove up and out stepped Tallulah Bankhead, all dressed up in silver foxes and with a lot of make-up on. She's awfully homely and looks just exactly like she does in the movies. The autograph hounds surged around her, and then the police stepped in and safely escorted her into the hotel. Her new play, "Foolish Notion," which Aunt Elizabeth saw in Detroit, opens tonight.

By late November my peculiarly carefree existence appeared to be on a settled course. Though I kept inspecting the list posted of those to be transferred, my name was never there. An officer informed me I'd probably remain at Tower Hall for "quite some time yet."

With so much liberty, even in practically free Chicago my money tended to run out; now I regretted having signed up for war bond purchases. But it would take months for an order rescinding the bond deduction to go through, so I did nothing about it. Instead, following a buddy's suggestion, I took a night job at the Railway Express station on Roosevelt Road. Wearing Navy jeans, sweater, and my watch cap, I lugged packages from one conveyor belt to another. Dusty, heavy work, mindnumbing and routine. Now with a Social Security number, I had joined the labor force of America in what seemed like the very bowels of commerce. We were temporaries, on late-night or early-morning shifts; it was understood that the Navy need not be informed.

The job didn't crimp my social life very much, as this letter indicates:

Nov. 20, 1944

Dear Mother,

. . . I planned on working last night, but things turned out quite differently. My friend Gordon . . . is a rather devout Catholic. Yesterday afternoon he was at church in the cathedral across the street while I was getting ready. He recognized the movie star Una O'Connor and had quite a talk with her. Her new play, "The Ryan Girl," opened last night. She invited him to bring me and come back stage . . . I don't know if you remember who Una O'Connor is, or not. I didn't at first. She's been in hundreds of movies. She's a frail, little lady about 55 yrs old, with bug eyes and a hawk nose. She's the indignant maid in most pictures, who's always scolding about something or shaking her finger at someone. She was that in "Christmas in Connecticut." She was one of the crazy sisters in "Ladies in Retirement."

The Servicemen's Center gave out fifty free tickets, so we had no trouble getting seats. The place was still half empty—mostly because Tallulah Bankhead's new play opened last night too.

The play was a stinkeroo. It really flopped. It was a low-moraled murder story, and June Havoc (Gypsy Rose Lee's sister) and Edmund Lowe were the principal characters. Una O'Connor was the maid, and the only good one in the cast.

. . .Backstage of a real theater is much different than the

movie version—especially the dressing rooms. [Una O'Connor's] was just a little room with a few chairs, a dressing table and a mirror with light bulbs all around it. She sat there with her make-up kit and was rubbing on cold cream as we talked. She was very gracious and talked a lot—about what we were interested in, where we were from, the acting business . . . After a little while we left, and she offered her skinny little hand to say goodbye. You couldn't help feeling a little sorry for her—even though she was an Academy Award winner and has made thousands, she still has to work hard every night to make a living.

We had just gotten out of her dressing room when she called us back saying she had promised to introduce us to June Havoc and Eddie Lowe but had forgotten.

Lowe had already left, and people were jammed into Miss Havoc's dressing room. We said never mind, that we'd have a hard time getting through to Miss Havoc, so we said goodbye again and left. I didn't particularly want to meet her anyhow, after [seeing] the character she portrayed in that rotten play.

Was I trying to defuse Mother's possible shock over my interest in meeting Gypsy Rose Lee's sister? Hoping to reassure her of my Sunday School goodness by pronouncing it a "low-moraled" play? Whatever, these postures indicate the sexual turmoil I was in. Many of my Tower Hall mates seemed further along than me, claiming to have lost their cherries years ago—though some didn't sound convincing, only the casual-acting jocks, who scarcely spoke of the matter. There was a certain calmness about these guys, amusedly aware of us kids left behind. They toweled dry in front of the mirrors, smug in their superiority.

One Monday night, on liberty and with the girls in the South Side apartment, I fell asleep on the sofa and didn't show up at Tower Hall until 8 o'clock muster. What a lot of knowing winks and teasing! I didn't confirm or deny. However, what was actually happening in my love life was depressingly the same. The girls I dated were matching my courtship rituals, both of us knowing all the rules and regulations exceedingly well.

With part-time work uncertain, I was often too short of cash to go out on dates. Although Christmas mailings increased the volume at Railway Express, extra hands were less and less needed. My buddies and I figured that perhaps discharged servicemen were being hired instead of us in our blue fatigues.

What then to do with my extra time?

Dec. 7, 1945

Recently we discovered a YMCA three blocks away. Every day we have liberty, we go over and have a workout. They have elaborate, expensive equipment, and we use all the facilities, weight-lifting in particular—following a scientific course and lifting a little more and heavier weights each time, to build up gradually.

This damp Chicago weather is good "cold" weather, so today I took my first ultra-violet sun treatment. Each treatment costs a quarter, and it doesn't take long to be nice and brown.

Then it was home for the holidays, Aunt Elizabeth arriving by train from Detroit, Aunt Anne from Worthington, Minnesota, all of us together at services in Christ Lutheran Church on Christmas Eve. I tucked into lavish home cooking and enjoyed a bit of rabbit hunting in the grove. Having dropped away from high school acquaintances, I felt awkward trying to look them up now, so I remained away.

After New Year's I was back in Chicago, gadding about. Dinner in a suburb with Grinnell friends, "catching up on the latest news. Then Ginger and her sister came over and we played bridge for a while. We had a hilarious time, and I finally got to Tower Hall about 3 A.M. This morning I slept till noon, so I'm not tired." And a few days later I watched Ethel Barrymore in *The Joyous Season* from the fourth row, on a free ticket: "You could see all her facial expressions; it was a beautiful performance."

But I longed to settle down to some serious work.

Jan. 26, 1946

Dear Mother,

This may be somewhat surprising to you, but I sent in my application to Chicago U. to take accounting. There were various reasons for this decision. I still don't know exactly what I'll major in. I'm pretty sure it won't be journalism or English, so I thought I'd try my hand at business to see how I'd like it in case I'll want to major in Econ & Business. Secondly, the U. has a reputation of being extremely radical in government and history and current affairs, so their course would be pretty tainted . . .

Who's the person writing this? I don't know him—can hardly explain him! Mother with her New Deal enthusiasms and her subscription to *The New Republic* in its radical editorial days must have been surprised to learn of this conservatism taint infecting me. Perhaps fear of the Russians or too many *Chicago Tribune* articles had gotten to me. Whatever the case, I braced for a course in accounting because I needed to arm myself for economic survival in the "real" world—which wouldn't be a life of constant theatergoing and dancing but probably a nine-to-five job in business. How grown up I must have felt, facing my options squarely and accepting a sober fate.

I still dreamed of becoming a writer and read voraciously, but little I'd set down on paper found favor with anybody thus far. In high school I'd enjoyed art classes too, but not enough to contemplate becoming a commercial artist. I'd been a success in a few high school plays and thought of an acting career, but even with only a handful of men on campus at Grinnell, the drama coach had passed over me when casting the part of Bramwell Brontë.

Better that I now present myself to Mother as the sensible young man she would be reassured to know she had reared: looking to his future in the marketplace, equipping himself with the skill of accounting. "If I am transferred and am very busy, I can still complete the course a year after my discharge." But where at Tower Hall would I study? "There are twenty fellows in a room about as big as the dining room and kitchen at home, so it isn't very peaceful around here." I'd have to haul my schoolwork to the Servicemen's Center library.

Everybody at Tower Hall had too much empty time and not enough money. Some of my bunkmates traveled in feral packs and told of rolling queers in the Gold Coast just a few short blocks away, where the rich lived. They boasted of how they could spot a homosexual by the foppish way he dressed or the ass-sprung way he walked. They'd let him lure them up to his apartment, but before he could try anything funny, they'd slug him, grab a radio, rifle his wallet, take any valuables around, and dash out. I was horrified by these accounts and astonished to hear them talk so blithely about their criminal behavior. Though they looked a bit sheepish and grinned and laughed among each other for reinforcement, they had only contempt for their victims and didn't think what they'd done was wrong. To their minds queers deserved such treatment because they preyed upon sailors. We all knew about "Lucy" in the chow line with his simpering, liquid leer; we tried to avoid being served by him, for he would grin and lick his lips at us. We made fun of him in private—and some of my buddies to his face—but I only felt a kind of fear and loathing of Lucy.

Then one day in Chicago I met a portly, youngish man who told me he wrote radio plays, and yes, his name was Norman Corwin. Why, I'd heard of him! He was a writer whose work I admired, and now I revealed my own ambition along those lines.

Where did we meet? It may have been on a streetcar or in a cafeteria, some public place. I'm surprised I wasn't on guard and suspicious, but the idea of becoming acquainted with a professional writer was too overwhelming. How much I needed to ask him! Such as, how did he get started? What did one have to do? When was his first big break? Were his plays aired from a studio here in Chicago? Yes, I'd very much like to visit a soundroom and be present for a broadcast (that would be something to write home about!). Back in his apartment he had radio scripts. Would I care to see them?

A cautionary thought popped up—was he safe? He seemed very friendly and at ease, almost offhand with me, as if we'd known each other a long time. Not on the make or pressing. So I agreed to go.

The street where he lived was very posh, on the Gold Coast, not far from Tower Hall. We rode a small elevator to his flat, which turned out to be only one room with a kitchenette, shrouded in drapes, quite dark, surely not the apartment of a successful writer. I knew at once that this man wasn't Norman Corwin. I demanded to see the scripts, but he tried to calm me down, saying we had plenty of time. He became more and more nervous because I must have looked terrified and ready to bolt.

No, I did not care for a drink; no, I would not sit. I realized I must have planted the name "Norman Corwin" on him myself, and he played along with the notion, seeing my gullibility. Now he was not about to let me escape without a struggle, which at this point was verbal.

I finally settled on the edge of a studio couch. Immediately he was right there next to me, hand on my thigh. I pushed it away. He went into a long explanation of why he wasn't in the armed services, something about his head, sudden brain-storms—none of it made sense, except I knew he was telling me he was crazy and that's why he was 4-F. A steady spiel but none of it added up. With an avuncular smile he scolded me for being closed in and unyielding, saying that when I was in the womb, my mother had had to "do" for my father, didn't she? During that time they couldn't have had sex in the usual way. I began to understand he was proposing fellatio (not that I knew the word), and he insisted there was nothing wrong with this. But for me the idea was so incredibly disgusting, I went pale and began to sweat. I wanted desperately to get out of there, but he'd locked the door behind us when we came in. (I thought at the time it was only what city people ordinarily did.) My buddies' tales of rolling queers got turned around with respect to the violence; I wondered if he might become abusive and out of control unless I was extremely careful. He seemed fanatic and demented, almost drugged with the notion of seducing me, and little of his talk sounded rational.

The radio plays: Where were they?

Oh, later, later. Now he would show me something special, pictures in a photo book that would really arouse me. Here, see how her legs are spread. She's really something isn't she?

A skater or ballet dancer. The pose wasn't especially erotic and I wasn't about to get excited. He urged me to lean back and unbutton my sailor flap, but I refused and told him to stay clear away from me. I couldn't figure how to extricate myself from this and just clutched his picture book, while he assured me he had only the kindest regard for me and didn't wish to upset me in any way. My pretty face had landed me in this fix—not the first time, but those other incidents at urinals or elsewhere had been fleeting. Never had anybody stalked me this directly.

When he moved to the far corner of the room, I kept him in the corner of my eye but didn't know what he was up to. He started making odd noises, as if he were being strangled. I glanced over: he was squatting there, masturbating. And just as I looked at him, he let out a groaning sigh.

I slammed the book shut, stood up, and said I *had* to leave at once. He adjusted his trousers and spoke calmly, hoped we'd meet again soon—would that be possible? He'd like it very much. I'd done him so much good, and he thanked me profusely. Could he see me again, he begged. To escape I said yes—give me a call anytime—and then he unlocked the door and I ran.

For days afterward I had scares on streetcars and subways, thinking I saw him, that he might still be after me. I told nobody of this incident, ashamed over having been taken in to the extent of going to his apartment. My bunkmates would have chided me for not stealing his watch at least or trying to blackmail him, saying I'd turn him over to the police. How could I have had a queer so much at my mercy and allowed him to get away?

The experiences I chose to write home about were quite different: a wedding, for instance, in Park Ridge, where I was the guest of Vivian from Grinnell. "I was having a gay time dancing with the pretty bridesmaids and other girls . . . About the only sailor there, and as the evening wore on, most of the people got a little high, which probably accounts for the fact that the orchestra played 'Bell-Bottom Trousers,' dedicated to me. A delicious buffet supper was served early in the evening, and the story of the wedding was in the Sunday *Tribune* and the *Sun.* So that's . . . how I crashed Park Ridge society." The next night, the Ballets Russes, again with Vivian; a few days later a hockey game, Montreal vs. the Chicago Hawks; and in between times I worked on the accounting course, often at the Chicago Public Library.

By attending to physical culture, as well, I could be sure of being ready in case I had to defend myself.

March 2, 1946

Dear Mother,

Wednesday I received a large box from Philadelphia, and inside was two sets of boxing gloves from Walter Schnerr [a language professor at Grinnell]. He had a new pair and sent me his old ones. We used to always box together last spring. So Thursday afternoon my buddy and I went over to the Y and had a fight. In the course of events I knocked his tooth out, so yesterday I bought two sets of mouthpieces, and the next bout is scheduled for Monday. He's a big six-footer, but doesn't know much about boxing, so it was a rather easy match.

What a tough guy I am—about time I remembered that. Uncle Jack loved boxing almost as much as baseball and had often told of seeing Jack Dempsey's fights while in New York.

However, in the same letter I took satisfaction in reporting progress with the accounting course.

> Friday afternoon I rented a typewriter at the library (a dime for thirty minutes) and typed up most of the work I've done. By Monday I should have two topics of the eight in the accounting course finished and ready to send off.

I received an A on the first part, a B on the second, and the professor wrote that I was doing well. I enjoyed the orderliness of accounting, the neat tucking in of arithmetical details to achieve a balance. Such calculations cleared the head and suggested a ladder of reason could scale any mathematical peak, unscramble any problem. But the feel of this activity seemed somewhat alien to me. My wild imaginings and unaccountable thoughts were not to be channeled into neat rows like this. I didn't believe the world could be reduced to these symbols—at least not mine.

By the middle of March I am still seeing new plays like *Dark of the Moon* and dancing to big band music. "After twelve most of the people left and when Tommy Dorsey started 'jamming,' the jitterbugs took over. I've become quite a jitterbug, by the way, and everybody really cut loose."

But living with a lot of coarse sailors finally put a pall over my otherwise entertaining life. I no longer had to lift weights or box to prove manliness to myself or others. I felt more comfortable with bookish kids who soaked up artistic experiences in galleries and theaters, who'd had a bit of education in these matters from school or home. But when needed I could ape the manners and attitudes of different types, could pass for anybody. Playing roles was one way to master situations. I enjoyed escaping into more lives than just the one given me—a trait that would later result in tale-telling on the printed page.

Some of my refined buddies like Gordon were even more sexually retarded than me and didn't go out with girls; he hoped to become a priest one day. I couldn't share with him my liberty escapades, mild though they were compared to those of my bunkmates. Once, two married men in their early thirties returned quite drunk from a night out. They taunted me about being a virgin still (though I denied it) and laughingly grabbed hold of my arms, putting fingers under my nose, telling me I was smelling a woman—wasn't it good? The odor interested me, though I was shocked to note their glinting wedding rings, which they'd worn even while visiting whores. I disapproved of their behavior, while acknowledging a certain pull, knew myself to be more like them than Gordon. Someday I would reconcile prudish Lutheranism with this other, though now my body urged me one way, my head another. It was a relief to be with guys like Gordon, for none of this could be talked about; there was just a neutering out of the male libido.

3 April 1946

Dear Lizzie,
. . . Tonight I moved into a smaller, but airier and roomier room where many storekeepers and yeomen are. There are only 8 . . . compared to the 21 in my old room. I sleep right near a window overlooking the lake . . .

In my next communication, I tell Mother that "all naval reserves will be in separation centers by August 20. So it looks like my Navy career won't take me any farther than Chicago." And, selectively informative about my social life, I recount a weekend with the minister's daughter, how we "rolled up the rug and started dancing." Couldn't imagine doing that in Reverend's living room in the Remsen parsonage, "but I guess it's permissible in a Congregational minister's living room. The folks, being a very romantic and understanding couple, went to bed at quarter to ten that night." I seem to be trying to convince myself that something significant happened that weekend, when the Bible fell on me in the midst of our near lovemaking. "Sunday morning we went to church, of course, and he had a very good sermon. With all his dignity in the pulpit, you wouldn't know him to be the same man." Clearly, I'm still hung up on the issue of things-of-this-world vs. the spiritual life.

In a subsequent letter I try to convey the many facets of the program I've worked out:

18 April 1946

Dear Mother,

... Tonight was my night for washing and writing letters,
tomorrow night is my accounting night at the library ... must
finish it before July 1 if I'm ever going to ... I also have been
doing quite a bit of writing lately because of the handy
typewriter here and the quiet office in the evenings, so, plus two
dates a week and my usual Monday night dinner-and-dusting
date at the girls' apartment on the South Side, my week is
usually pretty well occupied.

Thoughts of life after the Navy well up. "I'm anxious to get
home and see what clothes I can fit into and figure up my total
finances, start setting an approximate budget for the next fiscal year."
My accounting head put to use in my affairs immediately. Though
I'm saving no money now, I will need clothes, suitcases, a
typewriter—lots of things.

3 May 1946

Dear Mother,

... Last night I went up to Evanston to get a fitting for a
tailor-made suit. I'll surely need one, now that the boys will be
home to reclaim their clothes. [I'd worn my brothers' duds my
freshman year, since they were in the service.] ... The material I
chose is excellent—good for year-round wear. The color (and
you'll get a kick out of this) is blue. It's not at all the Navy blue
shade, but not too terribly light either. It has no pattern, so will
make a conservative suit.

By mid-May I'm convinced my Navy tour is about over. Time
to pack it in, a merry whirl, including an outing with my South Side
friends, whom I now have to share with five recently discharged
servicemen. "Since the girls were having trouble with their landlady
as it was, we decided a beach party would be better. So we got into
a big Buick and a Chrysler and drove to a rock promontory on the
South Side and sang to our hearts content." Coming up: Saturday
night, the St. Luke's nurses' prom at the Stevens Hotel ballroom; I
had reservations at the Edgewater Beach Hotel for dinner
beforehand. "My accounting has been terribly neglected, but I intend
to work on it tomorrow." I seem to have a miraculous way with

money, able to fund this hyper social life; perhaps I missed my calling.

In a letter to my brother Robert I brag about my ability to finagle whatever I want, such as an upcoming leave, though the lieutenant in charge of granting it was away for the weekend. I'd been working on an ensign, the officer next in line, who could influence the decision. "This came about with a little bargaining on my part. If he succeeds in getting me leave, I must turn over the names and addresses of all the girls I know in Chicago, so that he'll have a good time while I'm gone . . . since he's a good friend, I won't mind doing that, and I'm sure the girls I know won't mind because he is goodlooking, has a car and plenty of money. I've gone on liberty with him a couple of times, since he's about the same age I am." Which is to say, *I* should really be an officer too. I seem to have hold of a Billy Wilder movie script here.

The ploy worked and I journeyed home for ten days or so, returning to discover that at the end of June, Tower Hall would be closed down. We would be transferred to Navy Pier, where there were bunks for eight hundred men. Tales abounded: "It's partly open on top, and pigeons fly in and out and have nests in the rafters. They'll either have to build a new roof or supply us all with umbrellas." A larky tone, but at that point I hadn't heard of the wharf rats. Some sailors assigned to Navy Pier were already there. "As I was over talking to one of my buddies yesterday, a pigeon made a direct hit on his shoulder. The food, of course, is vile compared to what I've become used to here . . . Frankly, I'd much rather sleep in the hog barn at home."

With such a fate awaiting me, I could only key up my social schedule, dancing at the Aragon ballroom with my high school pal, Greenie; going to a ball game at Wrigley's Field; gambling at the slot machines one evening aboard the lake cruiser *City of Grand Rapids*. More dinners in the suburban homes of Grinnellians, and one evening a friend of my roommate's father blew into town, took us to "an ultra-classy hotel dining room," and "I noticed he paid the check with a $100 bill." Shortly thereafter there were visits from both my sister and brother Ken, when they came through Chicago.

"Networking" wasn't the term then, but I was shamelessly doing it. The reach of our family extended even to Chicago, with half a dozen introductions available, including a third-cousin in nurse's training, and one of my bunkmates hailed from a farm only eight miles from ours. A further ring consisted of high school friends and their contacts. I also leaned heavily on Grinnell connections, those hundreds I knew in my freshman year, plus their parents and associates. Should I continue to accumulate people this way, my Navy buddies would be next in the great chain of being, to be followed by new Grinnellians when I went back, then colleagues in graduate school, then the outer world—an integrated circuit system with reliance on the personal.

Now an old salt, my attitude had shifted from awe and respect for the Navy to open cynicism. In letters home I told about getting around service regulations, taking it for granted that my readers realized it would be sappy of me to stay straight with the Navy.

I viewed the decommissioning of Tower Hall as part of the comedy. Early one June morning we assembled on the gravel rooftop for a solemn ceremony to commemorate the good ship Tower Hall, which had seen her best days of voyage, played her valiant part in the great victory over the Axis powers. In summer whites I stood stiffly at attention among the line of sailors facing the incredibly long row of officers, their gold braid glinting in the sunlight. After appropriate remarks from the captain, a chaplain invoked Almighty God. Then we saluted as the flag was slowly lowered from the mast for the last time. Farewell to our brick ship adrift in the skyline of Chicago—this tiered barracks of shifting personnel, with its many absentees on almost perpetual liberty. Freeloaders all of us, courtesy of the U.S. taxpayer. The trumpet played taps; it was over.

But for me the charade was not yet over. Some officers decided I might be useful in their setup at Navy Pier.

2 July 1946

Dear Mother,

I'm getting settled here at the Pier and plan to call home tomorrow morning. The birds above me aren't pigeons—they're sparrows, and they chirp all day. Haven't seen any rats yet, but some of my buddies did . . .

In a few minutes I'll go down to the brig and pick up some prisoners to clean out this place. The birds are hopping around on the deck and sitting on the bunks, so you can imagine how clean this place is.

I was to serve as a clerical frontman for a clutch of officers living on fat per diems, plus hefty paychecks owing to their high rank. I somewhat resented their use of me this way. Proper discipline had broken down to such an extent that they even offered whisky in the middle of the day to me and my companion, sitting behind our typewriters.

An office of sorts had been set up in a kiosk in the huge, cavernous space, with desks and chairs, typewriters and paper, a telephone. But we had no legitimate business; there was nothing to do. Two of us were to be in the office during the normal business day, the other two spelling us from time to time. The phone almost never rang—only when an officer who was party to the scam called to get in touch with a crony or to warn us of an impending official inspector or once, a visit from big shots touring the premises in order to work out eventual disposition of Navy Pier. Mostly, it was extremely quiet in that well-lit island, with plenty of time to read books or, better yet, write. I rolled a sheet of paper into my machine and began to peck away, creating short stories, none of them about life in Iowa or even my Navy experiences but shallow imitations of *Collier's* fiction concerning city sophisticates. I hoped to sell one soon and ratify my secret hopes to become an author. Even my muse had gotten corrupted.

Without knowing winks or specific instructions from our collusive officers, I and my fellow clerk/typist Carl, from the Iowa Amana Colonies (who spoke with a distinct German accent and seemed like one of my relatives) understood that if a coverup were needed, we were to figure out something quick. We knew that the duty officer, who hung out somewhere down the Pier with a couple of other officers, should be called if any difficulty arose—outside inquiries or investigations as to what exactly was going on. Our job was to dissemble as necessary, to stall or make up some line that might sound plausible. But nobody came around to question just what our organization, Tower Hall Command at Navy Pier, really was.

Some shrewd officer back at the real Tower Hall barracks must have spotted my thespian capacities—an ability to charm and remain flexible in the face of the unexpected; altogether the right sort for this bogus setup. Alternately I played along or was resentful over being used. Once I passed the year-in-service mark, I figured I'd probably be immune to draft call-ups later, should hostilities break out between America and the U.S.S.R. I counted each precious day that earned college time toward a B.A. degree, which was how *I* was on the take.

"How's it going?" the duty officer might ask as he strolled by on rounds, poking his head in the door, looking sheepish. "Fine," I would answer, glancing down at dialogue just written: "'If you love me truly, you wouldn't deny me this small favor,' he said, to which she . . . "

Mostly my anger flared at night, for I hated trying to sleep in that enormous, empty place, with the sound of scuttling rats' feet on the floor and sleepy birds overhead banging around in the rafters. We used the second level of the three-tiered bunks, mattress on top as cover from bird droppings, shoes pulled up onto the springs of the first level so that the big gray wharf rats wouldn't chew the shoestrings or gnaw the leather. Caught in our flashlight beams, those rats scampered about almost as big as cats, their beady eyes showing little fright. What I couldn't do with my trusty .22 rifle, if only I had it handy!

Instead, I was occasionally armed with a Shore Patrol pistol slung in a holster at my belt, an SP emblem on the band around my upper left arm, although more often while overseeing work details of prisoners—a diversion from "office routines" which I rather welcomed—I carried only a billy club. Having had no target practice with the pistol, I probably couldn't have hit the rats anyhow. The prisoners whom I supposedly guarded on work projects were a harmless lot, most of them having been caught in some serious scrape such as a drunken brawl or an AWOL violation. Our hookup with the Shore Patrol, I deduced, legitimized our presence in the vast spaces of the Pier. Some specific reason for our activities could be pointed to, just in case.

On balance, the clandestine goof-off at Navy Pier was an appropriate but unworthy reflection of the original Tower Hall mission. Years later when Loyola University bought and rehabilitated the handsome neo-Gothic building, a story appeared in the *Chicago Tribune* headlined: "LOYOLA TAKES OVER SPY HEADQUARTERS" (or some such banner). An alert friend remembered I'd been stationed there and mailed the clipping with a quip: "So *this* is what you were really up to!"

It was at Tower Hall that the most difficult Japanese secret messages were cracked—encoded texts laboriously deciphered by America's best cryptographers. Countless American lives had been saved as a result, the war perhaps even brought to a close sooner. At the time I stood guard duty, many of the records, resource materials, and classified papers remained at Tower Hall. We paced back and forth in front of barred cages and sealed hall doors, wondering about those entire floors which were unused and off-limits for all personnel. The *Tribune* reporter particularly relished the fact that this vital aspect of America's war effort went undetected so long. Nobody suspected the true nature of what was purported to be a transit barracks, even though the decoding operation was underway directly across from the old Water Tower, one of Chicago's most visible and often-visited landmarks. Reading this, I was reminded of the diversionary scheme in Edgar Allan Poe's "The Purloined Letter," where the hidden missive is placed in such an obvious location that no one thinks to look there.

Now my tour of duty in the Navy is drawing to a close.

July 18, 1946

Dear Mother,

I doubt very much if they'll be done threshing by the time I get home, unless it's earlier than usual this year.

I'm very much relieved tonight after settling once and for all my heart murmur problem. This morning I was processed at the personnel office and told that I would be discharged at Minneapolis sometime before the 14th of Aug. This afternoon I had my physical, and got through without a hitch. The doctors were very thorough in testing hearts and spent a great deal of time on each person, so I don't see how he could have missed hearing a murmur if there was one. Apparently the murmurs have gone away, just like the doctor last year at Great Lakes said they probably would.

My thoughts could freely dwell on college, only a few weeks off. Would Lizzie please order a white shirt from Ward's, though I have six? "I'll need a white shirt every night for dinner at Grinnell . . . " And perhaps if my sister Ruth is in Minneapolis when I'm discharged there, she could direct me "to what stores are good." Since I continued to grow about half an inch a year (until I was twenty-one), much of the clothing I had wouldn't fit. My fixation on the apparel problem was indicative of my anxiety regarding the upcoming transition to mufti and the civilian world. I would be confronting a "normal" college scene with hundreds of male students instead of the mere twenty of my freshman year. Many returning GIs would be several years older than me; no doubt with deeper pockets.

A scrawled postcard sent from Minneapolis:

> . . . Discharged this morning and am spending the weekend here with Ruth. I plan on taking the morning train . . . on Tuesday . . . Clothes don't seem as scarce as in Chicago, but I'll find out tomorrow.
>
> My heart ailment showed up in the physical, so I'm applying for a pension. More about that later.
>
> Love,
> Curt

The government advisors said that since I didn't have a heart murmur when I was inducted but had one now—the specific hospitalization well-documented—compensation was surely due me. It was only right.

Last summer, lying in the contagious ward, I might fancy a red-badge glory about myself, receiving handouts from Red Cross ladies; but now in "real" life just what did my heart wound mean? Not a medical discharge—and yet a significant mustering-out entry regarding my health. Was my constitutional makeup so flawed that it might indicate an early death, like my father's?

At the Veterans Administration in Des Moines a week later, I was told I had a perfect case. A pension couldn't be denied me, though perhaps it would be at the minimum level since I wasn't badly off nor were my prospects impaired very much. Even a 10 percent compensation (which was the ultimate judgment in my case) meant that my educational benefits came under Public Law 16, not the GI Bill. For disabled veterans, one's specific career goal determined the extent of training, not length of time in service. If they approved of my objectives, the government would pay for all the needed schooling and provide me with larger subsistence checks than those accorded ordinary vets. Yes, my professional aim to become a college professor (thought up on the spur of the moment) would no doubt be deemed acceptable, since I had already proved myself academically with a year at Grinnell. American taxpayers would fund the necessary graduate school years, beyond the B.A. degree.

What a windfall! Mother need no longer worry about the education money running out or in retrospect question her early decision to spend more of her funds on the older boys than on me. I was now entirely self-sufficient.

With a beat-the-system mentality hardening my outlook, I could only gloat over my good fortune, unaware of the price in anxiety I would eventually come to pay. To have my body officially proclaimed flawed this young in life, eventually served as a depressant. I even began to wonder if the government truly bore any responsibility for my heart malady—if I hadn't actually enlarged my heart and perhaps caused the double murmur by overdoing it while training for the Drake Relays (in which I didn't, finally, participate). At the induction-center physical examination, the doctor had only briefly placed the stethoscope to my heart, much too casually.

I thought of those smart-ass Tower Hall officers who held onto their North Side apartments and indolent days for just a few more months. If they could see me now! I was pulling off a much larger scam and one that would no doubt ultimately cost the public much more.

Periodically in later years I became convinced that something was really wrong with me. I opted out of the weekly physical training periods required at Grinnell, explaining I was a disabled veteran on a pension. Intramural athletics were not for me. And though I loved tennis and didn't accept my infirmity while on the court, I later sometimes wondered if the arrhythmia I experienced meant something ominous. For years I was inconsistent in attitude, romantically adhering to my medical problem as if it were a special mark, then dismissing it in my quest to live normally.

At the time of my discharge in Minneapolis, a recruiting officer said I could be vulnerable to future military service, having been in only a year and a month. If that happened, wouldn't it be better to go into the Navy again instead of becoming a foot soldier? So I signed up for the Navy Reserve, believing it might be a protection.

When the Korean War broke out while I was in my second year of graduate work at Columbia, I received a pink-slip notification that an imminennt call-up was likely. Hey, guys, what is this? Didn't they

ON THE STOOP OF 85 LASALLE STREET, NEW YORK,
WHERE I LIVED 1950–51, WHILE ATTENDING COLUMBIA.

realize I was drawing a stipend as a disabled vet? What did they mean, I was soon to report for active duty? Wait till they listened to my heart!

But what did it sound like? I'd heard it pound in my ears while playing handball at the gym, and sometimes it beat on wildly after ardent lovemaking with my girlfriend, but that was only normal, wasn't it? I made an appointment with a cardiologist, who performed all the necessary tests. He told me there was virtually nothing wrong—maybe the slightest whisper of a deviation from the standard, but it meant nothing. I should live a regular life in every way. Yes, exercise all I wanted to, do anything. "Oh, I play tennis sometimes, but of course only doubles." No, no, he insisted. Do singles, work up a good sweat, use your heart, don't baby yourself.

"That's a relief to know," I replied, with decidedly mixed feelings—for would the Navy doctors agree with him? "If there weren't this problem with the Navy Reserves, I was planning on getting married in a few months."

Good, good, he replied with a smile. Lovemaking is the best exercise of all. And very good for your heart; just what you need.

The Navy for some reason forgot to do anything about its call-up warning; I never heard from them again. So I got married and went on with my life. The stipend from the U.S. Treasury kept coming on the first of the month—a very small amount, true, but it represented steady dream money. In *Bargain Paradises of the World* I read that two people could easily live on Montserrat in the Caribbean on $30 a month, so I thought of going off and writing a novel there, but never did.

To salve my conscience over that dubiously deserved pension, I told myself I was putting to good use the opportunities given me by this modest support from the people of the United States, who would be paid back in kind if I lived a productive life beyond mere self-gratification. I would engage in something socially worthwhile, if not noble. In due course I did become a teacher, arts administrator, and yes, at last a writer.

NOW THE FUTURE

Once the farmhouse is completely emptied, the barren attic, each wing a cavernous A-frame, seems a lot like the hayloft of the barn at winter's end: dusty, bigger than it looked when crammed full. Our voices echo, footsteps sound like the gait of giants. The round metal watertank, now empty of course, dominates as a fixture. Water used to be pumped up from the basement and the gravity-feed gave us our pressure—the same principle still in effect at my apartment building in New York City, with its huge cedar tank on the roof. Stripped of furnishings and clutter, I see clearly just how the mechanics of this house worked.

Lois and Rex realize I must fly back to New York soon and assure me that only minor details remain; everything has been sorted out. They will haul the last of the collectibles to that Le Mars consignment dealer. Lois says she'll send me a check for half of what it brings.

"Look, you don't have to think of that. Legally it's really all yours anyhow."

But by now we have far outdistanced legalities.

When Rex loads the pickup with a final collection of trash, the house will be ready for a "decommissioning" or "desanctification"— or were we accomplishing this by our actions here? No matter who lives in this building next, happily or not, our family emanations seem pretty well exorcised.

We shake hands and say our farewells on a cold, winterish November day, the weathered house a backdrop, merely a shell of its old self. Taking a last glance from behind the driver's wheel, I figure I'll probably be out here again sometime if for no other reason than to visit Lois and Rex. I recall what a woman at Uncle Jack's funeral said to me, with a mean, knowing smile: "Now that the last link's gone, guess you won't be coming around so much anymore, will you?

Lorne and Florence Nilles, Jack's neighbors and our current renters, repeatedly told me I could always put up with them, anytime I felt like a visit. Indeed, I might return in a few years to talk with the banker in Remsen who handled the rental contracts; catch up on the local news. However, I could imagine myself driving by on the road without turning in—just note the place through the trees, thinking with a little wonder: that's where I once lived. Whoever resided here then would very likely urge me to stop. Care to see what we've done to the place?

No thanks. For me it's a past clearly over.

For several years I stayed away, but the house in the meantime underwent a different fate from what was anticipated. No renters took over, no strangers lived in those rooms. Lois and Rex's younger son, Scott, married Jennifer soon after high school, and he asked to set up housekeeping on the farm. "Ever since he was a little kid," Lois said to me on the phone, "Scott loved the place. Then, too, he was so close to Dad. That probably has something to do with it. So I can understand why he wants to live there."

Possessing no capital, Scott could not undertake farming, even though he would eventually have access to 240 acres of land. Hundreds of thousands of dollars would be needed for machinery, plus a good credit rating at the bank. Instead, with his special training in operating earth-moving equipment, Scott found jobs on construction projects and did some long-distance trucking. Being handy and inventive like his Grandpa Jack, Scott proposed gradually fixing up the house, grounds, and outbuildings, adapting them for modern times. Jennifer soon became used to the luxury of ample house space and appreciated the extra empty rooms. A baby—Benjamin—arrived, and they were well settled in.

One spring after Easter I'm invited to spend a week as writer-in-residence at Westmar College in Le Mars. An "H" high school classmate (we were always seated alphabetically), who had recently sold his extensive meatpacking business and retired to Florida, made arrangements for me to occupy his house a few blocks from the campus, which he kept on for summer use. I accepted with pleasure, because it seemed an emotionally safe, neutral perch for me while I got my bearings again.

THE FARMHOUSE AND BARN
AS SEEN FROM THE FIELDS, 1978.

Once my college obligations are fulfilled, I'm free to explore familiar territories. On Sunday morning the pavement is slick with ice, but I maneuver carefully down Highway 3 toward Remsen; this was the bad-weather route we used to take to and from high school. I plan to attend services in Christ Lutheran Church, where no one is expecting me. I wonder if I will feel awkward or eerily removed upon entering Reverend's brick edifice, as if looking at my former life from far outside.

You know you're home when nobody you run into asks: "Why've you come?" or "What're *you* doing here?"

My presence is acknowledged by the parishioners with discreet nods and smiles but little surprise. One just takes up where one left off; it's always been this way. Amazingly, many of their names pop into my head, straight out of Sunday School nearly half a century ago. I settle into a pew next to Ruth Ann, widow of a seed-corn dealer; she had been particularly close to Aunt Elizabeth in the Women's Club, library, and other civic groups. Now she whispers to me before the hymn singing begins that everyone surely misses Aunt Anne's decorated Easter cookies—nobody's able to bake anything like them!

I follow the order of service printed in a *Bulletin* remarkably similar to the way these programs always looked. Toward the end of the service the new minister addresses the congregation directly from the pulpit, making various announcements and then warmly greets me by name. One of the young ushers whom I hadn't recognized must have alerted him. Now he even goes so far as to mention my writing, surely unaware that my first novel featured a rather weird preacher.

Although a prophet is supposed to be without honor in his own country, the adage didn't seem to apply in my case. I'd had intimations of that when I was invited to return to Remsen for their celebration of the national bicentennial in 1976. On that occasion I was placed in the backseat of a white Buick convertible, my name in big letters on the sides, and chauffeured through the streets while crowds lining the route shouted to me the titles of my books. Later, while downing beer and eating Luxembourger *tripen,* the captain of the Lippizaner horse patrol from Sioux City asked me who I was and why they were making a fuss about me. Somebody nearby spoke up, giving him details. The captain suggested I ride a white horse in the evening ceremony, which was to be held in the ballpark. Me on a white horse! My wildest fantasies of hometown acclaim would be incredibly, wonderfully realized. Unfortunately, the bicentennial committee thought my entrance on a Lippizaner stallion might upstage the Luxembourg consul from Chicago, honorary chairman of the event, for he could not ride beside me, being too old to mount a horse.

After services I join the congregation lining up for coffee, sticky buns, and the "fellowship hour," which takes place in an addition built onto the church in later years. I sit at ease among farmers I've known all my life, taking up the venerable acquaintances as if there's nothing much to be bridged by the time interval. We talk of the current drought, terracing and land conservation, government farm programs, and the state of the pheasant population. They ignore the obvious fact that my city life in no way resembles theirs, as if only the primary connections really matter: the fact that I remember their dead as they remember mine and that the rural world here keeps going on.

Afterwards, I drive out to visit Scott and Jennifer on the farm. Through the trees, the Victorian-style house looks almost modish, current fashions having caught up with it. The "heritage" plaque, marking the place as a hundred-year farm, is still prominently displayed. (Jack had proudly put it up shortly before his death.) The grove looks a bit skimpy at this season but several substantial oaks and locusts still stand, as well as young black walnut trees. Jack sold off the bigger walnuts at the time the region was plagued with "tree rustlers," who stole whatever timber might be valuable for furniture veneers.

Scott greets me as I step out of the rented car. Near him is three-year-old Benjamin on his tricycle, looking much like Lois at that age. In the house there's another baby now, Rebecca. Scott has given up long-distance trucking and also the construction jobs, which were too unreliable for steady income. He has joined the work force of a garment industry plant located in Marcus, about eight miles away, where Jennifer has been employed for some time. She operates a six-bobbin, computerized, Japanese sewing machine that stitches slogans and designs on Wrangler jackets, London Fog coats, and other apparel. She has an evening stint, working well after midnight; he's a plant supervisor on the day shift. Between them they trade off nurturing the children, sharing the cooking, cleaning, and doing what's necessary. The strain of it all lets up on weekends, when they often participate in her large family's anniversary parties or take a night out with friends. When I offered, on the phone from New York, to treat them all to dinner once I got there, Scott said: "Oh, we're all restauranted out!"

Now he asks, "Want to have a look around outside first?" He's a strapping six-footer and sports the obligatory beard for Remsen's upcoming centennial celebration. I recognize his suggestion as being much in the farmer tradition: The house is always secondary, compared to livestock, barns, croplands—which produce the wealth that makes family home comforts possible. Though Scott makes his living in an urban industry, he is still fashioned in the countryman's mold.

"I see the fields have moved in close." At the foot of the garden open land now begins and stretches to the horizon. "You've taken out that little grove."

"Those old cottonwoods; not much left of 'em."

The original eight acres Grandpa Harnack had set aside for house, gardens, orchard, barns, and feedlots, with groves on all sides had been reduced to provide more tillable soil. With access to earth-moving equipment, Scott was able to grub out the mulberry grove in one afternoon—which, with the stockyards plot that went with it, added a couple of acres to the cornfield. And those cottonwoods that used to dominate our view from the screened-in porch (we saw faces in the foliage and silhouettes of wild animals) were easily uprooted and burned.

Scott also did away with the icehouse and smokehouse, where hams and sausages once hung by their oily, good-smelling strings over apple wood smoke. Since Uncle Jack's death, nobody remembered the sausage recipes or even butchered on the farm, so there was no access to innards or meat scraps. Even the outhouse—"Mrs. Jones"—was gone, and some in my family might say it was about time. Although the farmhouse had indoor plumbing since the turn of the century, the privy had often come in handy, what with seven children, three parents, a hired man, and an occasional hired girl.

We saunter down to the two big barns, Ben at our heels; he's playing the part of miniature farmer, certainly dressed like one. The only livestock around is a flock of sheep in the lambing stage, which Nilles keeps here. We can hardly pull Ben away from that interesting spot. We walk up an earthen ramp into the hayloft, where a few clumps of musty bales from who knows what season suggest the original purpose of the place. A lot of English sparrows fly around overhead as if occupying a huge birdhouse. Floppy-winged pigeons fling themselves futilely against windowpanes high at the ends of the hayloader shaft.

"Ever notice this? Can you guess what it's for?" Scott uncovers an old implement which had probably occupied that dim corner for decades, though as children we somehow hadn't discovered it: a large, bark-stripped oak log with an axle running through its center, wheels attached to both ends. Scott tells me it's a handmade roller, which Grandpa must have used to flatten the coarse sod right after the virgin soil was first turned. We figure he probably fabricated the machine himself, out of a log from "back East." A real piece of

THE BARN, 1978.

pioneer history before our eyes.

And I thought I knew every inch of this barn.

"Ever come across those black walnut boards used to be around here?" I climb a ladder to an overhang, recalling devious hens of my boyhood who kept trying to hide their nests from me. Sometimes I wouldn't find them until the eggs were addled and I would have to throw them to the pigs below. One day, scrambling about, I noticed some inch-thick, heavy old lumber. Jack told me later what I'd found. Grandpa, a carpenter before turning farmer, transported these milled slabs from the Turkey River area where he'd grown up, with the idea of making furniture out of it in his spare time. So far as we knew he only completed a desk with a bookcase. The rest of the raw material was left here under dusty straw, forgotten.

Now we poke around a bit, sneeze. Yes, they're still here! Scott is excited over the find after hearing this history from me, and Ben fingers the dark wood as if he knows that he too must comprehend its meaning. Scott is learning, as I did long ago, that you seldom come to the end of discoveries, especially those in your own home.

I gaze out the barn door and everywhere I look there's something of mnemonic significance—even the slick, hide-scratched fenceposts of the cattle yard, the machinery rusting in the weeds. My later years of wanderings, from Iran to China to Europe have left scant residues compared to these from my youngest days. Only early memories could fully embellish that ordinary chicken-house ventilator I see before me now, puckered with holes from my BB gun. Here are my marks.

As we stroll away from the barns, I say: "Scott, you haven't disposed of much of Jack's old equipment, have you?"

He shrugs with a smile and admits that Rex has been teasing him about this too. All the implements I ever operated are still around in various stages of disintegration. Scott stores the more valuable curiosities of the past in the machine shed, including some of Jack's patented inventions such as the corn-picker attachment and a sidewalk snowblower; also a small garden tractor cobbled out of a variety of junk.

A grand exhibit of machinery stretches from the barns to the road and back again to behind the corncrib. I inspect the Wood threshing machine with its perch on the rear where I sat tending blower. The implement is a bastard combine now, having been converted by Jack when threshing machines became outmoded. Scott points out several corn shellers, including an ancient specimen with wood side panels now mostly rotten, as well as discs, harrows, planters, plows, drags, a sawmill, a corn elevator, and a few cannibalized tractors. "Actually, I hate to get rid of any of it."

"So I see."

"Then, too, maybe someday when I get the time, I can put a few of these back into shape."

JACK'S HOMEMADE COMBINE, CONVERTED FROM A THRESHING MACHINE, MAKES THE SIOUX CITY TV NEWS IN JULY 1967.

I'm a silent collaborator to such dreams and kick the steel wheel of an oats binder, which seems pretty much intact, although the canvas slatted sling that once stretched over the rollers is gone. The exhibit next to it is a mowing sickle for cutting slough grass and making hay. While operating it, if I came upon a meadowlark or dickcissel's nest I would quickly lift the scissoring bar and glide over the top.

"Could be of some value once they're fixed up," Scott says.

He clearly didn't believe in tidying up the past just to have it over and done with.

As we move toward the house, I spot the American Beauty rose bush, already green in the stems, making its annual spring comeback. This hardy, fragrant, thick-petaled pink rose likes where it is, planted in full southern sun but protected by the house. Jennifer is the fourth generation of women here to tend it, though its survival is probably due to needing almost no care—grateful for a pan of water thrown at it on extra hot days.

As we're about to enter the house, Scott speaks to Ben: "You can play outside, if you want." An area of the lawn has been securely fenced, where he could be alone without being minded. Under the syringa bush—our sweet-smelling mock orange—a refurbished sandbox contains strewn-about toys. I glance into Ben's blue eyes and figure I pretty much know this kid and what it's like for him to be by himself with the dog out here, encountering life in whatever bug, bird, or leaf it might be found.

"You like the color I painted the house?" Scott asks, looking up as we pause on the front steps.

"Yeah, it's close to the original, I think." We both know from a photo taken about 1907 and widely distributed in the family that the siding had once been dark with light trim, but one couldn't tell from the picture exactly what tints had been used. Scott painted the house gray with white edging—an improvement on the all-white it had been in my youth (and I had wielded a brush to help paint it).

He's pleased I'm not bothered by his having pitched out the decayed screen panels on the front porch. He touches the pillars, showing where he has rebuilt them.

"This is the way the porch should look," I say, nodding.

Jennifer calls us to come in out of the cold. I am company, invited to sit down in the front room. But first I have to glance around.

"We found the kitchen swing door in the attic," Scott says, pointing to the handsome door now in place, which had been removed perhaps in the forties during a kitchen remodeling. Rex left in the attic everything pertaining to fixtures of the house, including the dining room's globed chandelier. Unable to find the bottom bracket pin which once held the kitchen door in place, Scott ordered a modern substitute from the *Renovator's Supplies* catalogue.

"When company drops in," Jennifer says, "you don't always have the kitchen in such good shape." The door is closed now and I am not to see in there.

I'm still resisting a little the idea of plunking myself down in an easy chair and acting like a visitor, though I know it's my proper role. Instead, I gaze at the dining room floor and shake my head, muttering something about Grandpa's extravagance in laying down a floor of solid bird's-eye maple.

"That floor," Jennifer said, "it's the hardest thing to keep looking right!"

I suggest various polyurethene finishes. "Some of them don't have that bright shiny look. With a good cover on the maple, you won't have to wax or polish again."

Above us, the stamped-tin ceiling with its embossed squares has been scraped and painted, although because moisture always develops on the metal, I wonder how long it will last. I'm happy they didn't feel the need to "lower the ceiling" for heat conservation or were tempted to put up acoustical tile to effect a modern look. Scott says that new restaurants in California he's seen pictured in magazines install imitation stamped-tin ceilings to make a place look old. "But here we've got the actual thing."

No need for me to ward off a paintbrush attack on the burled pine woodwork throughout the house, for clearly Grandpa's love of natural wood still held through his great-grandson. Scott tells me that the wrinkled, crazed old varnish needs to be stripped, and he's begun upstairs in what will become Ben's room.

At last we move into the front sitting room, the original parlor of the farmhouse, which is now their living and family room, television set in the far corner. The foot-pump organ, which for a while had been in the local Heritage Center, is also here, more or less where it probably stood when Grandpa bought it for Bertha and Elizabeth to play.

"I'm sure this place doesn't look to you like it once did," Scott says.

I assure him there wasn't anything so special about our family belongings, just the usual middle-class furniture and oddments of the thirties and forties "used very hard, pretty much wrecked." Quality items like the rope-bottom maple bed and mahogany rocker had gone along with Grandpa, Grandma, and Bertha to the Remsen retirement house in 1920. Later an antiques dealer wheedled most of the good stuff out of Bertha, who mentioned to us how surprised she was by the prices they brought.

Jennifer runs upstairs, hearing baby Becky crying upon waking from her nap and finding herself alone. A few minutes later I make the infant's acquaintance and am told that her room is the little corner one, which was mine for a time.

"I always liked it up there, looking at the fruit trees." The windows had faced the orchard and grove.

"None of them are left anymore," says Scott.

"Not even the sour cherries?"

Scott shakes his head. The cherry trees, along with the dozen or more apple, pear, and plum, all died of winterkill, drought, and disease or were knocked over in storms or girdled to death by the deer, who in recent years huddled in the protection of the grove in winter. "Still got plenty of Juneberries, but how the heck do you prune 'em?"

"Nobody ever did. They were always about twenty feet high and hard to get at."

Scott mentions a landscape-gardener friend who has offered advice on what to do with the grounds, but Juneberry bushes were out of his ken too. Being so seedy, he wondered why anybody bothered with them. Grandfather had transplanted these wild berry bushes from the Turkey River bottom because he was fond of their tart, blueberry-like taste, though because of the seeds Juneberries were best when strained to make jelly.

These physical aspects of the land and house have become the enduring metaphors defining the sense of home which this place embodies for us, one generation after another. I hear Ben playing outside, calling to the dog; listen to the murmuring television with its volume low, like some monitor in the corner; sense the stately creak of the old house, which has contained so many lives over the years. Among family members little of this needs to be talked about; it's all understood.

Scott says he's thinking of moving the ornamental stained-glass windowpane from the bedroom upstairs to down here in the living room, where now there's only a leaded, beveled glass panel above the front window.

"Sure, why not?" I reply almost automatically, for I am no longer the caretaker here—even of memories. Whatever Grandfather had in mind by placing the prettiest window upstairs and largely out of sight, no one would ever know. In any case, the house's integrity of style couldn't be violated by the contemplated switch. Perhaps the window had been installed upstairs by mistake.

I find relief in abdicating my concern. The probability seems good, considering these small children just starting in life, that the old rooms will be filled with expanding personalties, youngsters acquiring their own set of memories and moving out and away from here. There will be life going on without me in its new ways, arising naturally out of what the past provides. If there's any immortality accorded us by way of such things, there could be no better version of it.

Sometimes I wonder if I tried to hold on too long. But if I had abandoned the attempt to understand the forces shaping me into the person I am, it would be like denying loved family members now dead—as if their lives in connection to mine had little permanent meaning, that given the permutations of anyone's character over time, their particular imprint is gone. Well of course it isn't. But I can't face in their direction while my own years overtake me and push me toward the many worlds elsewhere.

How very much is continually forgotten. I understand that in order to undertake the press of current living it's better that way. But now having looked back fully, it's as if easy access remains should I need to push open those once-familiar doors. For me the residue of this Iowa world will be located in those objects I accumulated over the years and still have with me, salvaged out of sentiment. And that's enough, knowing as I do that after me even these objects will have lost their histories as I now abandon mine.

Then Scott interrupts my thoughts. "Sure wish Mom hadn't sold all the furniture. Those antiques would look just right in this place."

"Oh, I don't know . . . " I can't think what to say.

"Jennifer 'n me didn't move here in time. To keep you guys from emptying the house," he added with a wry smile, "the attic and all."

We had robbed him of the chance to carry on with the weight of family accumulations, heavy in the attic. But would he have spent a life browsing through it as Jack and most of us had done, leaving the task of disposition to Benjamin, Rebecca, and additional children he might have? The attic never actually emptied, even by the year 2050 or later, when Scott would be old?

Perhaps it was not for me or anyone else to say the past was over. "How could we have known?" I answer and let it go at that.